Reading Between the Lines

Reading Between the Lines

BETTY JANE WYLIE

KEY PORTER BOOKS

Canadian Cataloguing in Publication Data
Wylie, Betty Jane, 1931–
    Reading between the lines: the diaries of women

ISBN 1-55013-637-2

1. Women — Diaries. 2. Diaries — History and criticism. 3. Women — History. I. Title.

PN4390.W95 1995   809'.89287   C94-932862-6

The publisher gratefully acknowledges the assistance of the Canada Council, the Ontario Arts Council, and the Ontario Publishing Centre.

Design: Jean Lightfoot Peters
Page layout: Heidy Lawrance Associates

Key Porter Books Limited
70 The Esplanade
Toronto, Ontario
Canada M5E 1R2

Printed and bound in Canada

95 96 97 98 99 5 4 3 2 1

Contents

*To Hope Davis
With Affection and Gratitude*

*And to the Bunting Institute
With Long, Fond Memories*

Preface

Kathleen Adams

Like most women, I kept a diary as a teenager. It was green fake leather with a ridiculous little gilt lock and tiny key that automatically rendered the contents by inference too frivolous and banal and predictable for words — that is, for any memorable words. And, in fact, any entries were doomed from the start, self-conscious and self-edited as they were. Small wonder I abandoned my first diary.

The adolescent diary stereotype involves large amounts of self-dramatization: hysterical emotion directed at rock stars, movie heroes, and boys; weekly and often daily switches of loyalty to female friends and of affection for boyfriends; exaggerated emphasis on the importance of minuscule skin blemishes; breathless reports of who said what to whom about-you-know-who; constant worries about one's clothes and hair; and the odd agonized but basically irrelevant reference to an essay or term paper that had to be done by yesterday — but who had time? These were the concerns of young female diarists of an earlier generation, but they are not so different on the surface from those of today's adolescent diarists.

Young black Latoya Hunter (b. 1978), entering Junior High in the Bronx, New York, in 1990, mourns the departure of a friend to another school ("The hardest part is not being together"); complains about the difficulty of communicating with her mother ("Parents just don't understand"); chafes at the boredom of school ("In every school there's a teacher that qualifies as a sleeping pill"); wonders at the fascination and elusiveness of boys ("I like guys. There I said it"); and wishes she were older. But she also reports on the "major risk" of walking alone at night in the Bronx, her determination not to fit in with the "dead-in-an-alley-headed crowd," her sympathy for a fifteen-year-old who had a baby, and her horror at a murder across the street from her house (someone she knew). Society has changed, but not diaries.

As I grew older, I found out that serious diaries were usually called "journals," generally by writers. I was told, as is every student of creative writing, to be sure to keep a journal to refine my thoughts, store my images, polish my phrasing, and cement memory. The journal would also serve as a commonplace book: a place to store other people's thoughts, good lines, great quotations, felicitous turns of phrase, and even, perhaps, the odd idea of my own.

So from time to time I did keep a diary, but it never served me very well as a commonplace book, let alone as a consistent record of my own thoughts and writing. After I married, I called my diary my "Bleat Book" because for years I turned to it only to bleat about how little time I had for writing. English novelist Virginia Woolf (1882-1941) commented about this tendency in her diary, that it often sounded only one note — of complaint — and so did German sculptor Käthe Kollwitz (1867–1945) in some surprise as she reread her diaries one New Year's Eve (1925):

> As I read I distinctly felt what a half-truth a diary presents. Certainly there was truth behind what I wrote; but I set down only one side of life, its hitches and harassments. I put the diaries away with a feeling of relief that I am safely out of those times. Yet they were times which I always think of as the best in my life, the decade from my mid-thirties to my mid-forties.

In 1973 I had made a New Year's resolution that I would keep a daily journal, one that was more than bleats, more than blow-by-blow accounts of the day's events. This new receptacle would contain, I hoped, mature, urbane, and witty comments on the life and times and people about me. I had a handsome, hard-backed blank notebook and a new pen with a flashlight in it so I could write when I woke up in the middle of the night without disturbing my husband, Bill. I began as one begins New Year's resolutions, with resolve and discipline. As the weeks went by, so often would I, without touching my diary. Then one evening in late April, Bill suddenly died.

Early the next morning I began my first serious diary. It was to prove my lifeline, my paper shrink, my source book, my closest companion, my confidante, my commonplace book, and my constant renewable resource.

Initially, it was the recipient of my grief. Often I didn't wait until the end of the day to pour out my feelings. Something would overwhelm me with pain, with the shock of loss, and I would run to the diary to agonize on paper and relieve some of the pressure of my grief, splotching the pages with my tears.

Gradually, as I kept on writing my own diary, I began to explore the diaries of other women. In 1976, *Revelations: Excerpts from the Diaries of Women*, edited by Mary Jane Moffat and Charlotte Painter, leapt out at me from a bookstore shelf. The treasures in this collection, insights into the life and mind and core of women, shatter your heart and stagger you with their truth. I was captivated. I began to search out the complete diaries, the original sources of the excerpts that particularly appealed to me, and went on from there, collecting other women's diaries. All the while I was still keeping my own, finding it continuously useful as a resource book on many different levels.

My father's mother kept a diary from the early days of her marriage. Everyone in the family became aware of it because in her latter years she used to boast that she had kept a diary for forty-some, fifty-odd, sixty-wow years. I knew I wanted to write, and I was fascinated to see what my grandmother had written in her diaries. I made it very clear to the family that I wished to inherit them. When she died, shortly after my first child was born, the diaries were duly delivered to me.

To my eager, unskilled eye they were merely appointment books, scanty records of luncheons and meetings, with brief attention to the weather. The only item I found interesting was her reaction to television, introduced late in her life. She called it "the new radio," not quite knowing how to account for the picture. As far as I could see, her diaries shed no new light on her life, offered no hints of an interior vision, no incisive commentary on her family, and no brilliant insights into world events. What a disappointment!

Later, when I told this story in an early report on diaries I was giving to a Women's Studies program, a history professor chided me after my talk, telling me that even seemingly banal diaries such as my grandmother's gave historians some idea of how people lived, what their social lives were like, and so on. But I wasn't a historian, I was a romantic. I was more interested in private visions, inner landscapes, personal discoveries. These were the treasures a diary unearthed, or so I thought at the time. I thought reading diaries should be like reading someone else's mail: the only words worth reading are ones that should never have been written, loaded with dark confidences and outrageous secrets. When it came to diaries, I was still a voyeur.

As I kept reading them, however, I began slowly to understand what women were discovering in their diaries, and how they stumbled on their truths. I learned many more reasons for journal-keeping and many more uses of the journal, both for their writers and for their unanticipated readers.

Not until I read the diaries of Emily Gillespie and Martha Ballard, edited by the social historians Judy Nolte

Lensink and Laurel Ulrich Thatcher, respectively, did I fully appreciate the insights that a seemingly humdrum diary can offer. These two social sleuths made me regret my careless rejection of my grandmother's diaries. Each has examined the life of a woman as seen through her diary, not only fitting her life into the pattern of her time, but also discerning her intentions, discoveries, and regrets and inferring her inner turmoil and hard reconciliations. These two diaries, published with their researchers' painstaking scholarship and sensitive interpretation, read like detective novels.

By the time I found Lensink and Thatcher, I was trying to decide on some kind of format for presenting my own delicious discoveries from diaries. In fact, I had been led by one woman's diary to a consuming project. In 1989-90, I was awarded a fellowship at the Bunting Institute, Radcliffe College, to research and write a play about Alice James, who was the sister of two of the (arguably) most influential Americans of the nineteenth century (William and Henry), and who managed to keep a modest diary in the latter years of her life. While I was at Radcliffe, I also took a journal writing seminar led by Hope Davis, an inspiration in herself. I was the only professional writer attending. My sister journal writers were women bent on exploring, discovering, and defining the self some of them feared they were losing. Certainly, a few of them wanted to improve their writing skills, but most of them were seeking something broader than that. I contributed, too, as we were all required to submit a weekly journal excerpt.

To a person as solitary as I have become, the sharing of my journal presented a frightening exposure, an exciting challenge, and a humbling experience. I was impressed by the wisdom and the felicity of expression of my fellow diarists and was grateful to hear their voices and to learn from their experience and insights.

As I shared weekly diary excerpts with the fourteen other women, I gathered samples and insights into contemporary diarists. I also interviewed my Bunting sister-fellows about their journal-keeping habits. All the while I kept reading every published diary I could find.

Delightful as it is to wander in and out of other women's lives, like the voyeurs we all enjoy being when given the opportunity, there's more to women's personal journals than history — public or private — more than the telling of gossip, though gossip can be important, more than the reporting of weather, or the recording of births and deaths. I began to discern some consistent patterns in women diarists' expression, and I started asking the same questions they were asking themselves. Why did they bother keeping a diary? And for whom? What did they think they were doing? What were they doing? What were they discovering? Is any of it useful? They were on to something, all of them, and interested enough to keep on doing it, over the years and over the centuries.

I think women diarists were trying to tell themselves something — for they were always their own first readers — something they couldn't put their nib on, something hiding there in the blank sheet of paper, waiting to be discovered and expressed, waiting to be told. Ultimately, they were telling themselves — us — what it's like to be human from a female perspective, what it's like to be a woman — in short, the truth about themselves.

I found over and over again that by the time I had experienced the life or part of the life of a diarist, I was loath to leave her. If she had stopped keeping her diary before her death, I tried to find out what happened to her. If her diary carried me to her death, I mourned her passing no matter how far back in the past it had taken place. I had trouble shaking her out of my mind and moving away from her into the present. All these diarists seemed to take on a larger-than-life prominence in my mind and a closer-than-kin significance. They were hard to leave; in fact, I haven't left them. Many of them have given me permanent insights that I now carry within me, and I count these women among my friends.

If I am so aware of a life leaping up from a repetitive account, of a psyche projecting onto mine from an accumulation of banal daily reports, of a vibrant woman with a real name and vital statistics, simply by reading a diary randomly created and haphazardly preserved, then obviously I have been touched. Someone has spoken directly to me. This is the power of diaries, of what is now called lifewriting.

A diary always tells of self; a woman's diary tells us not only of herself but of what it is to be female in a man's world. Often the diarist does not recognize or cannot articulate what that means; sometimes she makes a discovery after the fact through the very act of writing, or in retrospect in the re-reading of what she has written. We learn with her as we read and we make discoveries with her by reading between the lines.

From my Radcliffe diary:

September 29, 1989
There was a circular prism of light on the inside of my office building door this morning, about five inches in diameter. I wondered where it came from. I looked around briefly: nothing in the hallway, no windows, no crystal chandelier. Second time through I figured it out. There's a peephole in the door. The sunlight was beaming through it at such an angle as to hit the mirror at the other end of the hallway and refract back to the door as a magnified circle of coloured light — an accident of rainbow.

I am that peephole, I am that mirror. I am the peephole through which light shines, on a clear day, at the right time, at an appropriate angle, and meets with the mirror, that is, connects with an audience, the ultimate connector, reflector. My mirror beams back that eye-hole of light, enlarged, magnified, prismatically amplified to colour and illumine — not the world, but at least a small, dark hallway. So we shed light, or rather, let light pass through us, unimpeded but affected nonetheless by the mote in our eye.

Acknowledgements

This book has been a long time in the making and I have a number of people to thank for help along the way. Thanks to Tillie Olsen and Mary Jane Moffat and Jennifer Glossop, who lent me books; thanks to Shirley Reece and Per Syersted, who gave me books (Per gave me his last copy of Kate Chopin's *Miscellany*, which he edited; Shirley found amazing ones), and to Uma Parameswaran, who allowed me to steal a book from her. Thanks to the contemporary diarists who let me interview them. Thanks to the Schlesinger Library, Cambridge, Massachusetts, for the wealth of information and diaries I read in their stacks. And special thanks to my favourite bookseller, Charlotte Stein of Parry Sound Books, who was tireless and uncomplaining in finding and obtaining books for me.

I would also like to thank author Phyllis Chesler and all the publishers listed in the Bibliography, in particular The Feminist Press for excerpts from *A Day at a Time* by Margo Culley, copyright 1985; The University of Georgia Press for excerpts from *A Home-Concealed Woman: The Diaries of Magnolia Wynn Le Guin, 1901–1913* by Charles A. Le Guin; The Women's Press Ltd. for extracts from the diaries of Ruth Slate and Eva Slawson in *Dear Girl: The diaries and letters of two working women 1897–1917*, edited by Tierl Thompson, copyright 1987.

CHAPTER ONE

In the Beginning Was the Word

WHAT IS A DIARY AS A RULE? A DOCUMENT USEFUL TO THE PERSON WHO KEEPS IT, DULL TO THE CONTEMPORARY WHO READS IT, INVALUABLE TO THE STUDENT, CENTURIES AFTERWARDS, WHO TREASURES IT!

Ellen Terry

We begin with the verb *to be*. By definition, diaries are daily and immediate, written in the present tense. The present is all any of us have, but we also have, with hindsight and some attempt at preservation, what we have been and done. Diarists can weave in memory; they can also anticipate the future; they tell a daily, never-ending story.

Stories are a little younger than fire. Sheltered, fed, warm, keeping the wild things at bay with the flames, people began to tell one another stories; perhaps it was one person, by popular request, and everyone else listened. Initially a public skill, story-telling required an audience to complete the connection. It must have changed almost at once from documentary — the mere telling the tale of the hunt and the exploits of the tribe — to docudrama as the story teller embellished details, added colour, and stretched suspense. Thus began fiction, with its wavering lines drawn between reality and fancy. Stories rose shimmering with the heat from the fire and cast shadows as evanescent and eternal as smoke on the walls of the cave.

When the skills of reading and writing developed, the challenge arose: story-telling as art. Thoughts of posterity and immortality lured the story teller on. Writing was a private act with a public intent. Facts and history, myths and legends, allegories and parables, fables and fairy-tales were written down for wider and wider audiences to read, including future ones as yet unborn. The urge to write it down probably followed the ability to do so within the blink of an inner eye and the sharpening of a chisel, stylus, quill. The key word is *ability*.

The act of reading and the skill of writing are two different accomplishments and not necessarily automatically linked. By late medieval times, literacy in Europe was anything but universal, limited as it was to the upper ranks of the clergy, aristocracy, and landed gentry, all male. For the lower classes, writing was probably limited to the ability to write one's own name or scratch an X. Even lowly monks were often illiterate; illuminated manuscripts involved craft and skill, not necessarily literacy. From the mid-fifteenth century, the printing press would gradually change all that, but not in the way that is commonly supposed.

The Privileged Marker

> IN THE PAST ... THE PEN/PENIS HAS BEEN THE
> PRIVILEGED MARKER THAT WAS THOUGHT TO
> LEAVE THE MOST SIGNIFICANT TRACES ON THE
> APPARENT VACANCY OF NATURE, THE BLANK
> SPACE THAT HAD TO BE FILLED TO "MAKE"
> HISTORY.
>
> *Sandra M. Gilbert*

According to *A History of Private Life: Passions of the Renaissance,* the development of silent reading was of greater significance than the distribution of the written word. By the fifteenth century, people were reading to themselves. Roger Chartier, in his essay "The Practical Impact of Writing" in the *History*, summarizes the effect: "Finally," he writes, "silent, secret, private reading paved the way for previously unthinkable audacities.... Heretical texts circulated in manuscript form, critical ideas were expressed, and erotic books, suitably illuminated, enjoyed considerable success." To read ideas directly into one's inner, quiet space, to absorb an idea, this was the real beginning of the discovery of self, the first conscious distinction between your thoughts and my thoughts.

The numbers of readers began to grow in proportion to the amount of reading material available. But though tradesmen might do sums and yeomen might keep accounts, their writing ability was still limited to a signature. Among the male population, as might be expected, class differences dictated the degree of literacy achieved.

Women have been lumped together statistically, so they're harder to distinguish by class. Girls were taught to read, but seldom to write because writing was considered too dangerous a skill for women to possess. For one thing, wives could then write love letters to men other than their husbands, as Molière's seventeenth-century play *The School for Wives* warns.

In the sixteenth and early seventeenth centuries, an estimated 11 percent of women could sign their names. (Throughout this period, the gap between male and female literacy rates was as high as 25 to 30 percent.) However, as literacy spread, bright daughters of son-less fathers, or eager sisters of affectionate brothers, or clever wives of busy, absentee husbands were taught to read and write because it was amusing to see how much they could learn, or because the tutor didn't mind including them in some of the lessons, or because their skill was useful to the management of the household. While a few such women developed proficiency in their native language, none was ever permitted to study Latin or Greek at university because, of course, women were not allowed to attend university. An ambitious, curious woman might find a means to learn for herself or an indulgent father might amuse himself by teaching his daughter the rudiments, but the opportunities for a classical education were haphazard at best.

By the end of the seventeenth century, more women were literate — considered at that time to mean they could at least sign their names on a marriage register; not all signers were actually able to write. *A History of Private Life* reports data between 1500 and 1800 from three countries (Scotland, England, and France) that allows national generalizations. One example: marriage registers of the Church of England (which after 1754 required signatures of both bride and groom) revealed that, between 1755 and 1790, 60 percent of men were able to sign compared with 35 percent of the women in 1755 and 40 percent by 1790. Signatures collected about the same time in Scotland and France showed women's literacy rates at about 23 percent and 27 percent, respectively.

As for America, in the latter half of the seventeenth century in New England, 31 percent of women were considered literate (and 61 percent of men); that meant they could sign their own wills. The number of such literate women increased to 41 percent by the turn of the century (69 percent of men) and was 46 percent by the latter half of the eighteenth century (88 percent of men.) Other estimates give lower percentages; historian Barry Reay, for example, thinks that only 10 percent of women (and 30 percent of men) could sign their names by the time of the Civil War (1863).

This brief overview serves to remind us that writing was, at first, a rudimentary skill. Ordinary men used it to keep household accounts and family records. Writing as an act of communication and — way down the line — as an art form remained for many years élitist, rare, and precarious.

The first women diarists that we know of in any language astonish us not only for the mere fact of their literacy but for their grace and eloquence, even in translation.

Long before Western women took to paper, a few Japanese court ladies in the tenth century set out their private thoughts in what one of them called a pillow book, a receptacle for confidential thoughts, as private as one's bed; in other words, a diary. Its author, Sei Shonagon (963-?), served the young Empress Sadako from 990 to 1000. She recorded memories, poetry, and her thoughts on the conduct of love. As current today as she was then, she sounds a timeless sensuous note when she writes of the concomitant comforts of intimacy: "it is pleasant, too, on very cold nights to lie with one's lover, buried under a great pile of bedclothes."

Another Heian court lady-in-waiting, Lady Sarashena (b. 1058), chronicled her life from age twelve to fifty in *As I Crossed the Bridge of Dreams*. The *Kagero Nikki*, translated as *The Gossamer Years*, is an autobiography-diary spanning twenty-one years in the life of a mid-Heian Fujiwara noblewoman known only as "the mother of Michitsuna." It begins in 954 with her future husband's first love letters and ends with their almost-finished relationship, breaking off in the middle of a sentence.

What kind of compulsion was it that drove these women to write? Why did they learn to write *hiragana* (syllabic characters that are cursive in shape)? Sheer luck. Their menfolk had decided that *kanji*, the more complicated characters borrowed from China, were to be used only by male writers for serious writing, thereby leaving the ladies free to lick their pens with their vulgar tongues and bequeath us a rich legacy.

During the Hellenistic era in Greece and the late Republican and early Imperial eras in Rome, there were literate women who distinguished themselves, but accidents and neglect almost obliterated their work. For example, only remnants of the poetry of the great Greek female poet Sappho have survived, and those were in quotations and references by other (male) poets. A complete collection of her work, published in the fourth century, has disappeared. Towards the end of the nineteenth century, a few more pieces of her work showed up on papyrus fragments. It is impossible to know now whether any other women from that time and later kept diaries. My focus, therefore, will be on European and North American women whose lifewriting is available to us today, much of it by accident and not by design.

The first publicly literate European women were not as sensuous in their writing as their early Japanese sisters. English women in the late seventeenth century wrote radical religious tracts for public distribution, an act that often led to the writers' imprisonment. These spiritual autobiographies were seldom very personal and not very private. Less overtly intent on conversion, Susanna Parr (n.d.) in her *Apology* (1659) describes the death of her child (gender unknown) and reveals a personal attitude to God: considering the breach her child's departure made in her family, she thinks the Lord's loss was also a terrible breach in his!

Another account, *Heaven Realized* (1670), by Sarah Davy (c. 1639–1670), was "based in part on a diary kept to assess signs of her election or damnation, a practice much recommended by some sects" (Graham, Hinds, Hobby, and Wilcox, *Her Own Life*). The bereaved Hannah Allen (c. 1638–?) also monitored her soul after the death at sea of her husband. In a journal intended for publication, Allen kept a record of her "temptations and afflictions" as she fell into a "deep melancholy" — actually, a severe depression:

> May 26, 1664
> My language and condition grow sadder than
> before. Now, little to be heard from me but lamenting my woeful state, in very sad and dreadful
> expressions ... that now the Devil had overcome me
> irrecoverably and this is what he had been aiming
> at all along.

Not a whole lot of fun, but her plaintive reports clearly characterize what came to be known as conversion journals. The primary purpose in writing these journals was to produce a narrative of spiritual development. What is interesting about this soul's growth is that Hannah managed to make some psychological distinctions between her inner and outer lives and was able to break free of the never-ending self-recrimination that became a leitmotif of women's journals. Hannah Allen went on to a second, happy marriage, perhaps as a consequence of her rigorous self-therapy.

One of the first genuine diarists, Lady Margaret Hoby (1571–1633) of England, was also pious. According to American academic Harriet Blodgett, in her *Centuries of Female Days: Englishwomen's Private Diaries*, Hoby was initially impelled to write by the desire to monitor her spiritual and moral progress. Eventually, Hoby's accounting outgrew such reporting and became a running commentary on the highlights of the day's events. She may actually have begun her diary before 1599; part of the first extant page had been torn and the manuscript rebound, so there might have been more preceding. At any rate, her diary, from 1599 to 1605, is liberally interlaced with her religious observances and bears witness — in the truest sense of the word — to the spiritual tribulations and moral obligations of the godly but sickly lady. She attributes her physical suffering to her moral infirmity and considers herself justly punished by the Lord (August 17, 1599) "to corricte my sinnes, to send me febelnis of stomak and paine of my head ... so I might take better heed to my body and soule hereafter...."

But she is not above reporting for the sheer pleasure of it: "Mr. Hoby, my Mother, and my selfe, went to the dalls [*sic*] this day."

> October 5, 1603
> We had in our Gardens a second sommer, for
> Hartechokes bare twisse, whitt Rosses, Read
> Rosses: and we, hauing sett a musk rose the winter
> before, it bare flowers now. I thinke the Like hath
> seldom binn seene: it is a great frute year all ouer.

Another early diarist, Lady Anne Clifford (1590-1676), Countess of Dorset, Pembroke, and Montgomery, had legal matters on her mind and marital conflict on her hands. Lady Clifford was the daughter and only surviving child of the Earl and Countess of Cumberland. Her first marriage was to Lord Dorset, a man openly unfaithful to her (he once brought his mistress home with him for his wife to entertain as a house guest). After Dorset's death in 1624, her second marriage (1628) to the Earl of Pembroke and Montgomery was merely expedient as she hoped for his assistance in keeping her land.

In her "Day-by-Day book," her accounts of "falling-out" with her first husband sound a familiar timeless note. More outspoken and sexually frank than any of her contemporary and even many later diarists, Lady Clifford reports when her husband lay with her and, more interestingly, when he stayed away from her bed after an argument. As Harriet Blodgett points out, this isn't sex, this is sexual politics.

> May, 1616
> Upon the 15th my lord came down from London
> and my Coz. Cecily Neville; my lord lying in Leslie
> chamber, and I in my own. Upon the 17th my lord
> and I, after supper, had some talk about these busi-
> nesses ... where we all fell out and so parted for
> that night.

The battle continued:

> 1617, April
> The 23rd ... This night my lord should have lain
> with me, but he and I fell out about matters.

Lady Anne was a fighter. For forty-one years, she fought for the title to her family's estates, the Clifford lands in Westmoreland and Yorkshire. Her brothers had died in infancy and her father had willed the estates to his brother and male heirs rather than to his daughter, though the estates had been entailed originally to a child of either sex. The profligate Dorset wanted her to negotiate a cash settlement, which Lady Anne refused to do; this was the reason for their falling out. At one point, Dorset took their daughter away from her, in an effort to force his wife to his will. When she finally won the Westmoreland estates in 1643 (after her uncle's son died without heirs), she left her second husband and happily set about restoring her ancient castle, bounteous with her money and her wit.

Matriarchy and widowhood suited her best, until her death at eighty-six. She kept her diary to the very end, recalling with relentless *déjà vu* what happened on such-and-such a day forty, fifty, sixty years before.

Rarely introspective, she describes herself only once as lonely — "like an owl in the desert" (cf. Psalms 102:6). But she admits to "having many times a sorrowful and heavy heart" and reports that, at church one day (June 8, 1617), "my eyes were so blubbered with weeping that I could scarce look up." One of her chief motives in writing her diary may have been self-justification against terrible odds. The quiet paper may also have become an outlet for her anger and the release of that anger, a habit.

Spiritual exercise continued to be a reason for diary-keeping for the next few centuries. (As young women in nineteenth-century America, author Louisa May Alcott

[1832-1882] and her sister were required to keep diaries as a form of discipline and a means for their parents to gain an insight into their minds.) However, diaries also grew out of another form of personal writing. Like the first journals, early letters dealt with practical matters: records of household accounts or instructions to bailiffs. Many of these were written by the necessarily literate chatelaines of noble estates, accompanied soon by the wives of merchants and businessmen who used their wives as business managers.

Family members began to write letters to each other. This had nothing to do with literature; this was simple and private communication. It broadened and deepened in scope, from a pragmatic household account to something more intimate. The daily news easily expanded into a daily journal. In the New World in the nineteenth century, when women accompanied their husbands and families on the great western movement, their journals, in the form of daily never-posted letters back home, provided the most detailed chronicle ever set down of any historical event.

Chronicle, journal, daybook, diary, memoir, commonplace book — many people have tried to define what such an account is and to distinguish the fine points of difference among the names given to the keeping of one's private, quotidian history. Once that has been resolved, the harder question remains to be answered: what exactly goes into such a book? Consider for a moment the source of the word *diary* as a clue to the object's contents.

Easy to spot *diary* in the Latin *diarium*, "ration for a day," "a daily record," and the Latin *diurnum*, "a day," whence comes the English adjective *diurnal*, "daily," and the nouns, *daybook* or *diary*. Through *diurnal* we can glimpse *journal*, the French for "newspaper," the record of the day (*jour*), from Old French *jorn* (Italian *giorno*). The root is perhaps surprising: *diarium* and *diurnum* both derive from the Latin *dius*, "divine," the adjective of *deus*, "god," closely linked with *dies*, "daylight," "day," "duration of a day." The light of day is associated with the sky, with the source, with the god, the shining one (Indo-European *dei*, "to shine"). Thus by ellipsis and a leap, we arrive at the light within — the unspoken, unacknowledged inspiration and goal of the diarist. A journal, a diary, and a daybook are thus all one and (from the Latin *lux*, "light") a *luxury* to write.

Literate men have written and published diaries and journals for different reasons and different audiences from women's and under different scrutiny. Sharon Neiderman, in her book *A Quilt of Words* (based on women's diaries, letters, and original accounts of life in the American southwest from 1860 to 1960), points out that "men's journals and accounts were used as practical tools, as maps, to explore and conquer the territory. The journals of Meriwether Lewis and Zebulon Pike contain personal observation, but their intent is pragmatic, unlike women's accounts." These types of journals and the household records that men kept remained pragmatic, yet diaries were too beguiling not to be attempted. As American academic Thomas Mallon comments in his enthusiastic book about diaries, *A Book of One's Own*, "Writing books is too good an idea to be left to authors."

In one way, men had more to report: public events and exciting happenings, descriptions of their active lives, important records for posterity. Mallon lists diarists according to their subject matter, categorizing them as chroniclers, travellers, pilgrims, creators, apologists, confessors, and prisoners. His male examples outnumber the female excerpts by more than two to one, though he has been more generous than other anthologists. The point here is that male diarists have been published for "important" historical reasons and remain in print. Generalizations are dangerous; nevertheless, I suggest that the male journal has been less introspective than the female one, less a record of emotions than of events, and much less an apology than a justification of behaviour. If one were to judge by Samuel Pepys's diary or Frank Harris's *My Secret Life*, one could even suggest sexual braggadocio as a motive. Diplomats, generals, and explorers report their adventures, their strategies, and their involvement in events that affect history; these are the chroniclers and travellers. Priests and poets, writers and artists publish journals with their insights and notes, their spiritual and creative revelations; these are the pilgrims and creators. Diplomats step into the role of apologist and confessor as well, along with assassins and those who wish to justify their behaviour. Prisoners include not only the physically confined but also those who are trapped by dire circumstances or poor health. In any case, men's diaries received an earlier audience than did women's, because their subject matter seemed more important.

For Whose Eye?

Virginia Woolf

Sooner or later diarists ponder this question — after they have put a few hundred thousand words down on paper and the accumulation begins to look impressive. Somewhere between that evidence of production and the initial impetus lies some vague apprehension and later, even, an assumption of some other eyes than one's own reading one's words. If not at first, then certainly later, a commitment is made to a future putative reader, whether one's own grandchildren or a larger public.

First of all, right here, right now, a diarist is her own audience and it's a question of address: she wants to know what to call her private pen pal. Diarists frequently attack this initial problem in their opening words, just before or immediately following their statement of intent.

English novelist Fanny Burney (1752–1840) began her diary when she was fifteen years old and confronted immediately the problem of how to address her surrogate companion:

To Nobody, then, I will write my Journal! — since to Nobody can I be wholly unreserved, to Nobody can I reveal every thought, every wish of my heart,

with the most unlimited confidence, the most
unremitting sincerity, to the end of my life! ...
From Nobody I have nothing to fear.

Actually, "Nobody" was, first, her sister and, later, her father.
On her death, Burney left her niece what she called her
"immense Mass of Manuscripts, collected from my 15th
year, consisting of Letters, Diaries, Journals, Dramas, com-
position in prose and rhyme," which her niece promptly
began to edit and publish. Burney always had an audience
in mind.

A literary celebrity at twenty-five, Burney is credited
with having invented the domestic novel (her best-seller,
Evelina, or the History of a Young Lady's Entrance into the World,
was published in 1778); Jane Austen was one of her fans.
She filled her diaries with insider reports on the court (she
was Queen Charlotte's Second Keeper of the Robes, i.e.,
lady's maid, for five years); observations of the cultural,
political, and military scene; and, later, insights into a world
of exile, in France, from 1802 to 1812 (during the
Napoleonic Wars), after her marriage to Le Chevalier (later
General) Jean-Baptist Piochard d'Arblay.

American pioneer Emily Hawley Gillespie (1838–1888)
began what was to be her lifelong diary on her twentieth
birthday, careful in her establishment of place and person
and time, as if she were introducing herself to this entity
she addresses:

At Home at Father's
Diary — which may compose
reminiscences of the life, from day to day, of
Miss. Emmie E. Hawley.
A.D. 1858
Medina, Lenawee County, Michigan

April 1858

11th. Sunday. This I find to be my birthday. Arose this morning at six o'clock; set emptyings at 1/2 past six; sponged my bread at eight; had it baked by one; at ten Father was reading his Bible & Mother the newspaper. It is now two o'clock; it has been raining all the morning & is cold enough to snow. Mother says, "Here you are twenty years old & not married yet." "I think I feel as happy today as I should with a man and half a dozen children to bother me," I replied. Thus passes the first day of my twentieth year.

Six months later (October 11, 1858), Emily's diary had become "Old Journal." By New Year's Eve, it had become a friend: "Well, Diary, my cold is much better." This friendship continued for the rest of her life, through her marriage and move to Iowa, through the births of her three children (one died at birth), and through a growing estrangement with her husband. Emily's diary was her best friend and her only audience.

Elizabeth Smith (1859–1949) was one of the first woman doctors educated in Canada, a feat in itself at the hostile all-male medical school at Queen's University. She started her diaries when she was thirteen years old, being careful on June 2, 1872, to identify herself thoroughly:

> Elizabeth Elizabeth Elizabeth
> My Diary Elizabeth Smith

By June 9 she has established her connection: "Good night young diary, your [sic] more a note book than a diary."

As the pages accumulate, Smith, as every diarist does, begins to be aware of other eyes than her own gazing at them. She expresses this thought on March 30, 1873:

> Well, I think (there tis again now telling what I
> think) I had better not have written tonight for if
> any one should see it (Which I hope to Goodness
> will never happen) they would think but never
> mind what they would think there now stop stop.

This diary, which begins in such a self-conscious manner, records the emergence of a Victorian feminist and her growth as a woman. In later entries, Smith reports her ordeals at medical school and the changes she undergoes. She acknowledges these changes in herself and also her shift in audience in her last entry on June 22, 1884:

> It is a hard task this that I have set before me, not
> the writing in a diary as a résumé of what is almost
> painful at the least tiresome. I am a woman now, &
> so changed from that unsettled irregular immature
> young person ... [she describes finding her true
> love] ... so life is more & more — is fuller, wider —

deeper, thoughts & deeds are more so much more a diary would be irksome to me, so much repetition tho' the measure of it goes across the sea.

Smith's fiancé was studying in Scotland and her letters to him took the place of her diary.

Helen Ward Brandreth (1862-1905), the daughter of a wealthy family in Ossining, New York, was a private, unsung, young American woman whose "courtship diary" from January 2, 1876, to September 5, 1885, ceased when she married. She states both her intent and her method of address:

> January 2, 1876
> I have determined to keep a journal. I shall call
> it Fannie Fern [after a popular contemporary
> novelist]. My name is Nellie Brandreth. I have a
> low forehead, light hair and eyes and will be 14
> in February.

Later, as the writer becomes less self-conscious — or perhaps too self-conscious to call her diary Fannie — she changes the nomenclature: "I fear, dear old book, I will have to burn you in the end for you hold too many dangerous secrets" (November 25, 1881). She remains ambivalent; the "old book" becomes Miss Fannie again when she has news to tell: "Put on your specs, Miss Fannie Fern! There do you see what I have pasted on the top of the page?" (December 29, 1882). (It was the engagement announcement of a young man who had previously sworn eternal devotion to her.) In another moment of glee, when her true love has agreed to come to a ball, she writes, "O, Fannie, Fannie! do you see that?" (January 23, 1823). When Brandreth finally relinquishes the diary, she signs off with "dear old journal."

A lonely twelve-year-old American girl, writing under the pseudonym Kathie Gray (1864-?) and long forgotten but for an excerpt in an out-of-print book, gave her diary the title "Madame Looking Glass."

After two years of keeping a diary as an adolescent in her native Germany, American psychiatrist and psycho-analyst Karen Horney (1885-1952) gave it a name:

September 7, 1901
One thing more, my dear diary, I'm going to call
you kitten.

Another lonely, but remembered, teenaged girl also named her diary:

June 20, 1942
In order to enhance in my mind's eye the picture of
the friend for whom I have waited so long, I don't
want to set down a series of bald facts in a diary
like most people do, but I want this diary itself to
be my friend, and I shall call my friend Kitty. No
one will grasp what I'm talking about if I begin
my letters to Kitty just out of the blue, so albeit
unwillingly, I will start by sketching in brief the
story of my life.

The German-Dutch teenager Anne Frank (1929-1945) kept her diary while hiding from the Nazis with her family in occupied Amsterdam from 1942 until the Franks were betrayed by informers in 1944. She had no intention of showing "this cardboard-covered notebook, bearing the proud name of 'diary,' to anyone." After confessing her loneliness and naming her diary, however, she lets fall some awareness of a later, other audience — that unknown "no one" who will be unable to grasp what she's talking about if she is not properly introduced.

Another pre-adolescent girl emerged in 1993 who also has a harrowing tale to tell her diary. Zlata Filipovic, thirteen at the time of the publication of her book, has written a child's diary of war, the record of a young girl living through the recent devastation in Sarajevo. Self-conscious, goal-oriented (publication was her or her parents' hope), and not nearly as good a writer as Frank, eleven-year-old Zlata compares herself to the Jewish teenager and thinks she must name her diary as Anne did:

> Since Anne Frank called her diary Kitty, maybe I
> could give you a name too [there follows possible
> names] ... I've decided! I'm going to call you
> MIMMY

Young Latoya Hunter began her diary on September 10, 1990, as an assignment from a book editor as she entered Junior High. By September 30 she decides the diary has to have a name:

> I think I need a name for you. You've become like a
> best friend to me, you're someone I can talk to
> without being argued with. I think I know just the

name for you. I'll call you Janice after my best
friend from Jamaica ... so today I christen you diary,
Janice Page.

The Canadian writer Lucy Maud Montgomery (1874–1942), prolific creator of the beloved *Anne of Green Gables* and other girls' books, was an early and addicted diarist. She always had a sense of self in her address. On September 21, 1889, she had burned the diary begun when she was nine and at fifteen had begun a new one, intending to write "only when I have something worth writing about." Hence there are only sixteen entries at the end of the year. On New Year's Eve of that year, Montgomery reveals her chatty relationship with her diary, writing, "Well, journal, this is the last day of the old year." By April 1890, the diary has become "journal mine." Ten years later, she concludes this volume of her journal, by her own acknowledgement hard years, though she established her first success and reputation as a writer during them.

"Good–bye old journal," she writes. "You have been in all these long hard, lonely thirteen years almost my only comfort and refuge." Whoever else might read the diary some day, Montgomery remained her own favourite audience.

American poet Sylvia Plath (1932–1963) seems to require more of her diary than silent approbation. Planning her day, anticipating the arrival of something, listing her tasks, she demands a response: "Will it come and we do it? Answer me, book."

Harsh with herself, worried and careful about her own

"pale, hueless flicker of sensitivity" ("God, must I lose it in cooking scrambled eggs for a man...?"), Plath nevertheless depends on her diary as some kind of big, dumb, non-judgemental friend: "Goodnight," she writes in 1952, at the age of twenty, "Oh Big Good Book."

Few diarists before the present publication-hungry time thought beyond the moment in the heat of writing. The journal was simply a trusted, silent friend and confidante. However, one English woman, Ellen Weeton (early nineteenth century), mentally and physically abused by her husband, driven from their home, and denied access to her daughter, wrote her diary to her child as an explanation and defence. A well-to-do American woman, Ethel Robertson Whiting (1882-1974), began a diary when she was forty-two and kept it for fifteen years. She directed it from the outset to her unborn grandchild (*"Behold* your grandmother!"), liking the thought of being an ancestor and determined it would be a girl (it was, though she wasn't born until her grandmother was forty-eight).

Sometimes a diarist was persuaded by a fiancé or a husband to lay bare her private thoughts, that is, to allow him to read her diary, but this was a very special audience of one, by express permission. It's a surprise when the young French-Canadian Henriette Dessaulles (1860-1946) agrees to show her diary to her fiancé. This young man, the boy next door, four years older, was the subject and object of the girl's diary. Forbidden to socialize with him by her father and stepmother, Dessaulles, from the age of fourteen, had poured out her feelings to her diary.

Understandably, she has some misgivings about opening its pages to him:

> August 8, 1879
> I feel as if he were going to open up my heart
> to see what's inside and this almost causes me
> physical pain.

Alien eyes were unwelcome, not to say unthinkable. Paris-born Anaïs Nin (1903-1977) was an exception. Like Belgian-born American novelist and poet May Sarton (b. 1912) and American sculptor Anne Truitt (b. 1921), Nin always intended publication. Her diaries were her life work, and she not only published them regularly, but also kept the ones waiting in the wings in a bank vault.

Every diarist is her own first audience as she rereads her words. Often she will add in later comments, hindsight, or criticism of her earlier self. Almost every diarist does this.

However, French writer Marie Lénéru (1875-1940) didn't. A playwright and novelist, she is forgotten now but for a poignant journal, published in 1923 and long since out of print. Lénéru's first diary, begun when she was ten, records the onset of a severe case of measles, in April 1889. The introduction to her adult journal reports that after her illness the writing in the diary was totally different: the letters were a centimetre high, with three or four words to the line. The woman's journal begins in September 1893 and is a wonderful document. The miracle is that Lénéru could write at all. She was deaf and virtually blind, but indomitable. Lacking in self-pity, her diary attests to her courage and the doggedness of her spirit. She calls her journals a collection of "mental headaches" and assesses them with a writer's eye:

> March 13, 1900
> Shall I have the patience to reread them? What a question, never! ... if I did not ask myself, at the same time, what effect reading them would produce on others. I shall do nothing to have them published, but I want them to be publishable. I confess cynically, that I need other people because, at bottom, they are all there are.

Lénéru is an exception. Most diarists are their own most faithful readers. The major reason they don't burn the evidence before they die is that the journal represents a piece of themselves they are not ready to part with. They read and reread compulsively and sometimes in the harsh perspective of their own hindsight will rewrite large sections of earlier diaries, changing or omitting names to protect the privacy and reputation of others. Irish playwright Lady Augusta Gregory (1852-1932) did this towards the end of her life: "And just now my back aches after some hours of going through these diaries, striking out what is not worth reading or might give pain."

A diarist does not usually undertake this task unless she is aware of possible publication. Some diarists, if they live long enough, manage to edit themselves, copying and destroying, cutting and correcting as they see fit.

Sometimes they resort to a simple form of censorship: they tear out pages. Lady Gregory did this, as did the best-known of the Civil War diarists, Mary Boykin Chesnut (1823-1886), for a different reason: to present herself in the best light as she fought her own war for the Confederation. English socialist Beatrice Webb (1858-1943) did it, exercising her right as a cool editor of her diaries before publication. English novelist Barbara Pym (1913-1980) also did it to protect herself in a more private way. For whatever reason, these diarists reveal that they were aware of the risks of exposure. A diarist can't be too careful. The life she reveals might be her own.

Pages Torn Away

> WE ASK WHAT HAPPENED THEN. WE FIND NO
> MENTION. LOST, DESTROYED. PAGES TORN
> AWAY. DAYS MISSING. WE FIND DOCUMENTS.
> SHE FINDS LETTERS. DIARIES.
>
> *Susan Griffin*

Most diarists seem to agree that a certain amount of reticence is in order, in case anyone finds the diary. They describe their precautions, hiding or locking away their journals to be safe from prying eyes. A very few resort to a real code (usually easily cracked), but many have a code of their own — subtle hints, ellipses, or deliberate omissions that force us to speculate or make educated guesses. As we have seen, some number of diarists in their later years report pulling out and burning pages or recopying them.

Rarely, however, does a diarist destroy her entire diary. She simply neglects to tell all and leaves us wishing she had.

Surely one of the chief pleasures of reading other people's diaries is learning their secrets; it's a pity when they close up. On the other hand, the reticence of an earlier, more closed method of expression can be tantalizing. Reading between the lines, rereading after other facts are revealed, breaking the diarist's code, and perceiving other facts or contrary emotions with hindsight or with outside knowledge of her life and times, the reader begins to feel like a detective.

The question remains: how deep is the diarist's anxiety that her private papers remain private? Sometimes the concern is obviously in direct proportion to the nature of her confessions. I interviewed a contemporary diarist, a lesbian, who told me she never felt safe about her diary or free to write whatever she wished until she finally moved out of her family home to live alone. However, even with what may be considered a "safe diary," a woman may still refrain from telling all. Some confessions are too sacred to be entrusted even to a private diary, especially — the fear is always present — if it should fall into the wrong hands. This decision not to tell all is repeated in different centuries for different reasons, but it's always self-censorship and it stands as an obstacle between us and the diarist's full communication.

Lucy Maud Montgomery was a voluminous diarist. Even without the childish diary she destroyed (which she later regretted doing), and even with all the editing and abridging she did herself, her journals fill ten legal-size volumes of about 500 pages each, spanning the years between 1889 and 1942, in all nearly two million words. Yet it would seem that even she pulled back from telling all, both as a child and as an adult:

> Monday, January 20, 1890
> Mollie and I have made a decidedly startling discovery about some of our little personal affairs.
> I am not going to write it down because it is a
> dead secret.

Mollie was Montgomery's "greatest chum," Amanda Macneill. The boys called them "Mollie and Pollie" and the two little girls had sat together in school since they were "teeny-weeny tots." The dead secret was a joke, a mystery dangled in front of a boy to intrigue him. In later years, Mollie was a disappointment to Montgomery and she didn't hesitate to call her a "dead and buried friend of youth." On the other hand, taking on a self-imposed challenge to analyze herself (December 13, 1920, aged forty-six), Montgomery begins by doubting her ability to disclose everything:

> I do not believe any human being can — or would
> if he could — make a thorough and absolutely
> frank analysis of himself or herself.... I could not,
> even in these diaries which no eye but mine ever
> sees, write frankly down what I discern in myself.

Always there is this discreet silence, an automatic muffling that affects women even in their private pages. This is more than self-censorship — it often amounts to an outright denial of fact.

New England midwife Martha Ballard (1735-1812) expanded her account book with its case reports of births and payments into a fascinating diary, which she kept for twenty-seven years. We learn a lot about her life, family, and community, but it is evident that she censors herself. She refuses to dwell on her friction with her son and daughter-in-law, preferring to report only the good news. Likewise, the young English working-class feminist Ruth Slate (1884-1953) censors the telling of her fiancé's misdeeds, even in her own private space:

> Saturday, 13 March 1909
> A stormy interview with Wal [short for Walter] — a troubled, sad, sad walk — a more pacific ending. Wal told me what I knew but could never quite face. I cannot write of it here in case this book ever gets before other eyes than my own, but I went to bed smarting with agony for which there seemed no relief.

The problem women have with this kind of reporting is twofold, both external and internal. They fear alien eyes, but they also fear their own admissions. If they have this kind of trouble in the telling, how much more will the reader have in the accurate reading? Women have always tended to speak in code, whether in direct speech or in their diaries and written communication. By code, I don't mean the complicated ciphers used by the English writer Beatrix

Potter (1866-1943). (Potter's editor, Leslie Linder, tells how he broke the code in his introduction to her journal.) Many diarists use initials for the people they refer to most often, less as code than as a shortcut. Potter, however, a scientific researcher in spore development, as well as a writer of children's books, kept a journal from the ages of fourteen to thirty in her own privately invented code-writing, thereby making it very clear that she intended her diary for no eyes but her own. That kind of conscious code was very different from the oblique codes resorted to by some women diarists.

Not even aware of what it is, they practised something like synecdoche — taking the part for the whole. What diarists tell and what they leave out, what they infer and what they imply, construct an iceberg of communication, with much more under the surface than is apparent above.

Southern belle and rabid rebel Mary Boykin Chesnut, living in a hotel in Montgomery early in 1861 while her husband, James, attended the Confederate Provisional Congress, provided a salon where the key men of the new government and their wives gathered to gossip and plan. A witty, handsome woman who was childless, she loved being in the centre of things, to stir them up; in her diary, she often bemoans her husband's less impulsive behaviour.

On March 29, 1861, she reports that Mr. Chesnut made himself "eminently absurd" by accusing her of flirting with John Manning, governor of South Carolina and one of the richest men in the South. Using the name as a flag, we watch for its appearance: tea with Manning, and others, on

April 1; breakfast on April 2, when he brought her a bunch of violets; breakfast again on April 3 "with John Manning, who made better jokes than usual." A round of excursions and visits on the fifth and sixth ended with "the pleasantest time with John Manning" — and some other men. The war news was "rampant" all the while. At breakfast on April 7 with a group that included Manning, Mary Chesnut reports that Mrs. M[anning] has written for Mr. C[hesnut]'s likeness as she wants to begin a flirtation with him.

April 11, 1861
Yesterday dined with Manning, Cheves, &c, had the merriest time. Who could imagine *war* began today....

April 12, 1861
[After a night of cannon roar when Mr. Chesnut had ordered the first gun fired]
What scenes.... My husband — dined with us — looked so well in his uniform & red sash — rushed off to get an order somewhere.
Today Miles & Manning breakfasted near me. Manning got up & came to me — said we must be friends & not quarrel because he was all day to be before the fire of Fort Sumter & left a message for his wife....
Good news. Nobody hurt on our side.... To night — tonight — Oh my Soul!

To Gretel Lainer (a pseudonym for an unknown Austrian teenager whose dates are also uncertain), everything has a double meaning. Her adolescent diary, first published in German in 1919 and praised by Freud, is about the discovery of sex — "the facts of life." Obsessed, she is too embarrassed not to use a kind of code (and her translator follows suit); example, *p* is for *period*. She thinks the world communicates to her in similar fashion, that everything has a double meaning, and she is both terrified of and fascinated by everything she is learning about her own burgeoning sexuality and about what goes on in other people's lives.

> June 1
> It's awful; it's quite true then that one takes off
> every stitch when one is madly fond of anyone. I
> never really believed it … but it's true. [Gretel and
> her sister Dora stood at the window in the maid's
> room and watched a young married couple across
> the way.] She was absolutely naked, lying in bed
> without any covers, and he was kneeling by the
> bedside quite n—— too, and he kissed her all over,
> everywhere!!! and then he stood up and — no, it's
> too awful, I can't write it, I shall never forget it.

Gretel decides then that she will never marry because then "one need never undress." And so with women's diaries: the clothes don't come off.

Sex as a subject has been prohibited among women for centuries, and female diarists have been no less restrained when confiding in their diaries. Only in this century has death usurped sex as the big conversational taboo; previously women could speak and write copiously of illness and death while remaining virtually silent about sex. One presumes they knew what caused babies but they never referred to it; even when they were in childbirth they called it being "sick" or "awake all night." As for birth control, lactation and abstinence seemed to be the most effective means of holding off babies, for a while. Or else, as American historian Elizabeth Hampsten reports one woman writing to a friend (she in her turn repeating her husband's joking advice), a woman should "wear a long nightdress with a drawstring at the bottom and a lock and key." In her book *The Feminization of American Culture*, Ann Douglas points out that "external taboos and internal anxieties" barred women from "elaboration on the overtly sexual acts of impregnation and childbirth." They focused instead on illness and death, being "more interested in the moments at which crude energy failed than in those at which it accelerated."

Although taboos about sex, childbirth, and menstruation used to limit a diarist's direct expression, it's interesting to note what isn't said as well as what is. Emily Gillespie used three exclamation marks to indicate her periods. She was not the only one to use a code to keep track of these cycles. Some historians think now that editors in the past have eliminated diarists' mysterious notations. Whether comments or codes have been excised or not, it's a certainty that all these women knew more than they were saying.

Until this century when more reliable methods of birth control were developed, most married women were either pregnant or lactating for the greater part of their adult lives, and some of them had short lives because of that. If they didn't die in childbirth, they died of puerperal fever, breast abscess, prolapsed uterus, and, surviving those, of exhaustion, having fed their tired bodies inadequately and worn them out with back-breaking work. The only female diarist I've found who is wordy about sex and birthing, specifically about the trials of her pregnancies, is poor southerner Magnolia Le Guin (1869-1947). In the summer of 1903, after five pregnancies and with four living children, the thirty-four-year-old woman fears she is pregnant again. She feels rotten and fearful, and it helps her to write it down:

June 2
I am not well. I have been feeling real badly about a month and instead of getting better I am very much afraid I am going to feel worse. The Lord only knows the depth of my trouble over this sickness and to what heights my fears attain as to what the sickness may terminate [in].

I trust, hope, and pray for better things in regard to my health than what leads me to fear....

I pray from noon till night that this cup will pass from me. Lord thou knowest the anguish of motherhood.

June 6 or 13
I've never had to wean a baby as young as 12 months but I fear that will be Ralph's fate — and his second summer — the worst in a child's life.

Life is a duty — bear it
Life is a thorn crown — wear it.

I fear the thorn-crown is coming to me.
Heaven help me for all the trials that is to
come upon me.

In other words, Magnolia Le Guin is pregnant again, and nursing was not an effective means of birth control.

Selectivity as well as reticence shapes the contents of a diary. Like sundials counting only the happy hours, some diarists prefer not to dwell on the dark side and so gloss over their troubles. The future Canadian doctor Elizabeth Smith, out in the world at the age of nineteen and working as a schoolteacher in Speyside, Ontario, begins a banal report:

January 22, 1878
Nothing much to write tonight. This life like most others will become in some way monotonous. There are some things which will always prove a mine untold in depth which makes me content. There is no truth like God's truth and no comfort like His. Experience is a rough master but It proves a sure one of which to learn that God helps those that help themselves, and if you want a thing well-done do it yourself. They say a self made man has a rough fellow for his teacher but they might add a strict one and a sure one.

The inexperienced young woman was living in a boarding house with strangers, coping with an ungraded class, and feeling homesick and exhausted. Yet the string of clichés, old saws, tired maxims, and sampler philosophy could have been written by anyone — until she pulls herself together and gets personal. Only then does Smith describe her quavering voice as she goes through the opening exercises at school:

> I'm sure my voice is very broken and my eyes
> moist when I finish the Lord's Prayer and raise the
> desk-lid to conceal my face while I steady my
> nerves.

Turn-of-the-century American novelist Kate Chopin (1851–1904) had her share of blues and also used clichés to dismiss them. "Heigh ho!" she writes in one of her rare entries in a diary on February 24, 1869, when she was eighteen years old. "This is one of my blue days." She claims herself a creature who loves amusements, yet she questions the effects of too many parties and balls. Her age, her gender, her position in society do not permit her questions to be taken seriously. "Heigh ho!" she writes. "I wish this were the *only* subject I have doubts upon." Better to hide in cliché, formula, and ritual.

Many diarists were hampered in their free expression by a shortage of basic material. Time and energy were in short enough supply; paper and ink were even more limited. Constant interruptions clipped the diarists' words briefer than their accustomed laconic style.

American pioneer women heading west on wagon trains stretched paper and snatched time from the gruelling demands of the journey to write their diaries. At the end of the day, when the wagons, horses, and men stopped, after they had driven the wagon, gathered fuel for the fire, and tended the children, the women cooked and cleaned up, washed and mended, set the bread to rise, rising themselves in the night to prepare it for breakfast, and kept a diary in their spare time. (Many of the diarists were young unmarried girls who had more time.) Paper to write on was a luxury, an indulgence whose value had to be conceded by the men.

Keturah Penton Belknap (1820-1913) began to keep a journal at the age of fifteen in Ohio, where she was born. When she was nineteen, she married George Belknap on October 3, 1839, and two weeks later left Ohio with her husband in a two-horse wagon bound for Illinois where news of a land purchase drove them on to Iowa. She lived with her in-laws until her husband built a house of their own. Over the next few years, Keturah bore four children, two of whom died in infancy. Then her husband caught the "Oregon fever," and in March 1848 they left Iowa to move farther west with the children and her in-laws.

Belknap kept on writing her diary from the wagon train. Like some other pioneer diarists, she mentions how hard it is to get paper and how she must use it sparingly and well. She writes, "For want of space I must cut these notes down [and] will pass over some interesting things." She doesn't mention where she obtained the paper. She was short of time, too, and sleep, but the writing was a precious priority and she feels a pang when she must leave it:

April 10, 1848
Daylight dawned with none awake but me. I try to
keep quiet so as not to wake any one but pretty
soon Father Belknaps [*sic*] voice was heard with
that well known sound: "Wife, wife, rise and flut-
ter" and there was no more quiet for anyone.

Some sheets of women's diaries and letters surviving from
this period are difficult for historians to decipher today
because often when a paper-poor writer finished a page,
she would turn it sideways and write across it, running at
right angles to the script already there.

A number of diarists have been concerned with their
pens and ink. One can understand why when the ink
freezes over, as it did in an earlier century in North
America. Other diarists merely complain of scratchy nibs.

Some women were able to keep a diary by sheer chance;
some had to overcome their own lack of skill, literacy, edu-
cational level, time, and energy, or cope with constant interruptions, their lack of freedom, their own caution, and
their scanty, uncertain equipment. As if all these obstacles
were not hazard enough, what miracles prevented the
destruction or loss of the diaries after a writer's death?

They seem often to have survived by accident rather
than by design. The earliest manuscripts of some diarists
have turned up among yellowing archives in family trunks
and libraries on both sides of the Atlantic. Even the work
of writers who intended their work for publication has not
always been entirely salvaged. New England spinster Alice
James (1848-1892) left her diary as a specific bequest to her

brothers, considering it her life's work. Her companion Katharine Loring accordingly sent a copy to the four of them after Alice's death. Novelist Henry James read his copy, admired his sister's style and wit, and burned it, urging the others to destroy theirs as well. (He burned a lot of his own papers, too.) Rob James saved his and left it to his daughter; an expurgated version of it was published in 1934. Not until 1964 did Henry's biographer Leon Edel turn to Alice's diary and publish a complete edition.

Arthur Ponsonby, a collector and reviewer of diaries, has commented that no editor can be trusted not to spoil a diary. Certainly I have come across some censored, tampered-with material. The most famous deletions discovered recently are those made by her father to the diary of Anne Frank. Interested readers may want to look at *The Diary of Anne Frank, The Critical Edition* (1989), prepared by The Netherlands State Institute for War Documentation, with the cuts and edits plainly indicated. Frank may have wanted to protect his wife's memory by cutting Anne's descriptions of her parents (e.g., "Mummy is tiresome, Daddy sweet and therefore all the more tiresome"), and possibly to leave a more flattering picture of himself.

English poet Ted Hughes cut portions of the diary of his wife, poet Sylvia Plath. In the introduction to the poet's journal, Frances McCullough, Ted Hughes's co-editor, explains: "There are quite a few nasty bits missing — Plath had a very sharp tongue and tended to use it on nearly everybody, even people of whom she was inordinately fond.... So, some of the more devastating comments are missing ... and there are a few other cuts — of intimacies — that have the effect of diminishing Plath's eroticism, which was quite strong."

Ted Hughes also explains: "The last of these [the notebooks] contained entries for several months, and I destroyed it because I did not want her children to have to read it."

One of the strangest diaries I've read is the result of a reverse problem: not expurgation but addition. The journal of New Zealand–born British writer Katherine Mansfield (1888-1923) is almost factitious, created after her death by her husband, John Middleton Murry. He took her spasmodic diary entries and interleaved them chronologically with her regular letters to friends and her almost daily letters to him during their frequent, long separations and produced, if not a journal, at least a partial record of a writer's mind.

Perhaps more diarists could ensure their privacy, safety, impunity, and honesty by doing what Margaret Fountaine (1862-1940) did. She took care that her diaries would survive while preserving her reputation and that of anyone mentioned in them who might be offended. An English lover of butterflies and men, Fountaine bequeathed her butterflies to the Castle Museum at Norwich, with the condition that the black metal box accompanying her collection not be opened until April 15, 1978. This treasure box contained more than a million words of her diaries, along with photographs, drawings, postcards, and pressed flowers, covering sixty years of Fountaine's life, her travels, and her remarkable love affairs. So far, two volumes of her travels and love affairs have been published.

The diaries of English novelist Virginia Woolf could easily have been destroyed during World War Two. She and her husband, Leonard, had evacuated to their country place at Rodmell when their city home on Mecklenburg Square in London was bombed. Woolf grieved that they had left their city address, until she saw that it had been reduced to rubble. On October 20, 1940, she describes the mess at Mecklenburg Square: "Books all over dining room floor. In my sitting room glass all over Mrs Hunter's cabinet — and so on. Only the drawing room with windows almost whole. A wind blowing through. I began to hunt out diaries." By that time the writer had thought of making something out of her material, perhaps "an article of these 15 odd diaries." She couldn't have foreseen what an industry they have turned into, though she had begun to suspect an audience for them, as even the most private diarists do, sooner or later.

Not to Be Taken Seriously

WHY DO WOMEN KEEP DIARIES?... THE FORM HAS BEEN AN IMPORTANT OUTLET FOR WOMEN PARTLY BECAUSE IT IS AN ANALOGUE TO THEIR LIVES: EMOTIONAL, FRAGMENTARY, INTERRUPTED, MODEST, NOT TO BE TAKEN SERIOUSLY, PRIVATE, RESTRICTED, DAILY, TRIVIAL, FORMLESS, CONCERNED WITH SELF, AS ENDLESS AS THEIR TASKS.

Mary Jane Moffat and Charlotte Painter

Another barrier to the survival of women's diaries lies in the perception of them by the diarists' menfolk. American academic and feminist Carolyn Heilbrun has commented on the kind of silencing of women that men achieve when they trivialize the talk of women "not because they are afraid of any such talk, but in order to make women themselves downgrade it." A similar male attitude prevails concerning women's diaries, with an additional undertone; men are sometimes jealous of the time journals take and the attention they receive.

A lonely woman whose husband doesn't talk to her will turn to her diary for companionship — that's almost a given. But a woman who clearly prefers her diary's company to her husband's is suspect and resented — by her husband. Emily Gillespie never deviated from her lifelong diary habit, begun before her marriage and sustaining her as her marriage broke down. Her devotion to it was another source of annoyance to her husband, James. She reports a jibe he makes at it (and then excuses him for it):

> Tuesday, May 17, 1864
> I asked James to get a few sticks of wood to bake
> by. he said "Write it in your Diary," for tis the first
> time, he is not very well.

As time goes on, Emily uses the diary almost as a surrogate for her husband. She reports another comment:

> Thursday, February 3, 1876
> James says I may write in my Diary, to have warmer
> feet when I come to bed.

These little scenes, of course, give us clues to a disintegrating relationship, but they also illustrate a man's attitude to his wife's diary. Most women who persist in keeping a diary during a marriage learn to be discreet about it and put it away when the man comes home. It's like women's gossip: he just wouldn't understand. Women actually have a real story to tell in their newsy gossip, chatty exchanges, and seemingly inconsequential diaries. Beneath the surface details are clues for survival and a world of psychological truth.

Until this century, when historians have turned to women's diaries for revelations other than pragmatic facts, men have tended to patronize them, ignore them, or reject them as banal and commonplace, in short — trivial. When examined, neither women's diaries nor their gossip turns out to be as trivial as a casual reader or a man might think.

The noun *trivium*, meaning "a place where three ways meet," comes from *tri*, three, and *via*, road — three streets. The plural *trivia* initially meant the three classic subjects of study (arts, both mathematical and linguistic, science, and philosophy) — for men only. We take trivia now to mean trifling, unimportant. The adjective *trivial*, still, according to the *Oxford English Dictionary*, means "such as may be met anywhere, commonplace, familiar" — not necessarily unimportant. In ancient times, a three-faced statue was placed at crossroads. It represented Hecate, or Trivia, goddess of the moon, of the underworld, later known as goddess of witches. As they reclaim a female language, women writers, diarists, and gossips should remember the significance of trivia.

As for the charge against women of gossip, again reconsider language. The noun *gossip* comes from *God* plus *sibb*, Old English for kin. A gossip originally was someone spiritually related to God, eventually a godparent, a female one, although initially of either gender. Gossips were a woman's female friends invited to be present at a birth; by association the word came to be related with the "idle talk" they indulged in, the "tattle ... mostly about other people's affairs," and so gossip became the subject and the verb.

Gossip, men would say, is what women do best, but this is where we come to a parting of the ways. If gossip is the expression of the trivial in its truest sense, then indeed women do it very well. "The assumed triviality of gossip has constituted one basis for attack on the activity," writes feminist academic Patricia Spacks, who has written a book called *Gossip* about gossip's influence on literary forms. "It might equally well supply a ground for defense." Gossip is the stuff of domestic history and the very substance of female networking.

Gossip spreads the word that Mrs. Wan's baby is sick and Mrs. Fertile just had twins, that Mr. Bottle hasn't been seen for a few days and Mr. Driver was in an accident, not killed, but badly hurt, and Miz Blue has a black eye and Mr. Feckless has lost his job, and Rosie's looking rounder these days, oh, and Ol' Lady Ache's front porch is falling apart, and maybe — someone needs help.

Without gossip the community would not be as protected and safe as it is. Gossip provides the scraps of life that are stitched at the sewing bees and the quilting parties, and the strawberry picking, and also at coffee breaks, hair-dressers, car pools, and Home and School meetings, as well as in diaries, when report time rolls round. Diarists are very good at gossip.

Here's Southern diarist Mary Chesnut:

March 6, 1861
Yesterday evening Mrs. Fitzpatrick, Scota Holt & Mrs. Elmore called. Mrs. F noisy as ever, taking me to [t]ask for saying she received with Jeff Davis. Then Judge Withers introduced me to Judge Hale a congressman, but the man listened to Mr. Mallory. I wish Mr. Mallory would not tell me so much of his flirtation with Mrs. Phillips. I do not think it is as innocent as he pretends, but it's none of my business. Mr. Mallory told tales & amused us until half past ten — when, he & I being left alone, I came up stairs. So much for a man's having a bad reputation.

March 12, 1861
Browne was talking last night of Miss Lily McAlister & Bergmans' marriage — she old, ugly red haired, clever & an heiress, he handsome, worthless, young, with only twelve hundred dollars a year. She only lets him waltz with her — hangs on his arm all the time. Browne says if ever a man earned his money, Bergmans does!

Many diarists tend to use bad-news gossip as a kind of cautionary tale and try to draw a lesson from it, if possible. In her diary for July 9, 1806, New England midwife Martha Ballard relates the horrifying details of a mass murder in her community and prays, "May an infinitely good God grant that we may all take a sutable notis [*sic*] of this horrid deed, learn wisdom therefrom." Western pioneer Emily Gillespie reports a suicide, and then a woman going mad and adds her homily (errors hers):

> July 28, 1877
> Mrs Smith call here this evening. she said they had taken *Mrs Brook* to the *Insane Asylum* last tuesday ...
> [next day]
> ... I only wonder that more women than do do not have to be taken to the Assylum, especially farmers wives, no society, except hired men to eat their meals, hard work from the beginning to the end of the year, their only happiness lies in their children...

Gossip is like a quilt with random scraps stitched together to make a whole, to make sense of the whole. The scraps may include local events, anecdotes, and tidbits of useful information. Magnolia Le Guin's notebooks include recipes and cures, another commonly shared topic, and — lest we think professional writers are above gossip — here's British novelist Barbara Pym taking note on an April day in 1955: "At the Women's University Settlement I see Miss Casson wearing a dress that I sent to their jumble sale some time ago — and very nice it looks."

Diaries overflow with gossip, providing the clearest picture any social historian could want of people firmly rooted in their time and society. Gossip is information at its most basic level, the raw material of documentary, demographics — and fiction. On a personal level, gossipy diaries give us the information we need: how people lived, what they did, how they saw themselves. We can also discern how men perceived women and how male attitudes and male language have shaped women's lives.

CHAPTER TWO

Lifelines

> THE FEMALE "I" WAS ... NOT SIMPLY A
> TEXTURE WOVEN OF VARIOUS SELVES; ITS
> THREADS, ITS LIFE-LINES, CAME FROM AND
> EXTENDED TO OTHERS.
>
> *Domna C. Stanton*

Women's diaries have been called lifelines. The term aptly encompasses three essential ideas. There are the literal written lines of each woman's personal life story. There is also the idea of life-saving: the lines thrown from ship to shore to hold the ship, or from the ship to a diver or to someone drowning in deep water, are the means by which someone may be saved who cannot survive by her own efforts. And there is the lifeline in one's own hand, supposed to indicate the vitality and length of the subject's life. Women's lifewriting constitutes all such lifelines.

Although begun as a mere record of household accounts or a report of spiritual progress, as time went by, the daily journal was to become the receptacle for more emotional confessions. The lines are thrown out for the writer to catch — or is she caught? Sooner or later, most diarists succumb to the addictive nature of their activity. When she was sixteen, English political writer Beatrice Potter Webb (1858-1943) expressed the attraction on March 6, 1874: "Sometimes I feel as if I must write, as if I must pour my poor crooked thoughts into somebody's heart, even if it be into my own."

A Woman Who Loves

THE MORE SHE FEELS CHERISHED BY SOMEONE SHE LOVES, THE LESS NEED A WOMAN HAS TO WRESTLE WITH QUESTIONS OF HER SELF-WORTH. THE MORE SHE HAS COMMITTED HERSELF TO THE WELFARE OF ANOTHER, THE LESS NEED SHE HAS TO PONDER THE EXPRESSION OF HER OWN DEEPER SELF. A WOMAN WHO LOVES MAKES THE NEEDS AND WISHES OF THOSE SHE LOVES A PART OF HER OWN IDENTITY.

Ruthellen Josselson

And so they were married, and lived happily ever after.

Any number of diaries, begun when the diarist was in her early teens or younger, end when she marries. She gives herself and the responsibility for her happiness to the man who takes over her person and her life. Some diaries, in fact, are simply the record of a courtship and nothing else.

Helen Ward Brandreth bids a formal farewell to her journal (aka Fannie Fern) shortly after her marriage:

September 5, 1885

Dear old journal, good bye. I will never care for
another; as for you, I sign myself with my dear
new name:

HELEN WARD POTTER

Young Henriette Dessaulles, whose entire journal was a
surrogate for the long-forbidden boy next door, prepares
to leave it as she approaches her wedding day to him (he
waited for her to grow up):

May, 1881

When I was a child I really enjoyed writing. I
wrote this famous diary then, of which I have
destroyed the first few notebooks.... I feel less and
less like writing.

I'm about to begin a new life, a life partly hidden by a mysterious veil that no one lifts for me. I'll
discover it with him, my beloved who will be my
husband. How strange it is to be entering an
unknown world that everyone seems to be familiar
with and yet no one speaks to me about....

I don't think I've mentioned yet that the wedding, *my wedding*, has been set for the 19th of July.
Eight weeks from now.

It is almost unbelievable.... I can't really say that
I'm impatient; no, it's lovely, it's perfect the way it
is, but I'm happy to be slowly moving towards this
wedding which will make me his. Yes, I'll be his!
That's what is so wonderful!

Other early diarists express similar joy. American novelist Kate Chopin writes that she has let her "book" (her diary) go for a year without even missing it, so intent has she been on other things:

> May 24th, 1870
> Pardon me my friend, but I never flatter you.... All that has transpired between then and now vanishes before this one consideration — in two weeks I am going to be married; married to the right man. It does not seem strange as I thought it would — I feel perfectly calm, perfectly collected. And how surprised every one was, for I had kept it so secret!

"Latter day fate ordains," wrote Beatrix Potter to her diary in 1894, "that many women shall be unmarried and self-contained, nor should I personally dream to complain, but I hold an old-fashioned notion that a happy marriage is the crown of a woman's life, and that it is unwise on the part of a nice-looking young lady to proclaim a pronounced dislike of babies and all child cousins." Her life was never thus crowned, but like most women she believed in marriage as many still do, or try to. Other diarists express a certain amount of apprehension concerning marriage, but hope for the best.

Lifelong American diarist Emily Gillespie, for example, declares surprise and some disbelief:

> Sunday, September 7, 1862
> James was here all day, most & evening, too till

eleven. Can it be that next week Emmie is to be a bride? Yes, yes, if James fulfills his promise....

Even at the moment of closure, that is, of marriage, the page trembles. Is this really a happy ending? Is it, indeed, an ending? What lies ahead? Will we live happily ever after?

As writer Katherine Mansfield comments in her diary, "The Fairy Tale [is] our history really. It's a tremendous symbol. The Prince and Princess do wed in the end and do live happy ever after as king and queen in their own kingdom. That's about as profound a truth as any." Women have been fed this "truth" for centuries so that it is difficult for them to conceive of alternatives. American sculptor Anne Truitt agrees: "The idea of being protected by men dies hard."

Another diarist expressed her longing. The young American Azalia Emma Peet (1887–1973) knew exactly what she wanted:

April 12, 1913
The prince does not come. I wonder if he ever will and if he does not is it my fault?

November 23
And still the prince waits.

December 14
And still the prince lingers. I guess he is lost and will never come.... I want the prince but maybe a career will do.... But the prince, I want him.

1914. January 4
Still no prince!

January 8
Yesterday I learned that the prince (was he the prince?) is married.

August 3
Oh! I do want the other life — the right prince and the dear babies. Are they ever to be mine, I wonder?

December 6
The prince doesn't come. Now and then I think I catch a glimpse of him but I soon find out my mistake.

1915. February 28
And when the prince does come, let him show me the true meaning too. Oh! may he come soon. I am so very much alone, after all.

August 3
I am lonely to-night. I wonder if it is the prince I'm wanting.

August 15
I want the prince to come. No I am not lonely but I feel as if there was a big something in life that has as yet been denied me. When will he come? Never?

September 17
I wonder if the prince is waiting to be so very much needed. I wish he would come. I am twenty-eight years old and I feel as if I had been a wee bit

robbed because this experience has been denied
me.

December 25
Mary [a friend] has a nice home, a good husband,
two darling babies and — is very much tied down.
I have none of the aforesaid and am quite free —
yet I would exchange with her in a minute if the
"right prince" asked me.

Peet gave up waiting for the prince and left her home in
Rochester, New York, in 1916. She went to Japan, where
she worked as a missionary for thirty-seven years, being one
of the last Americans to leave the country in 1941 and
boarding one of the first boats back to Japan after the war.
She stayed there until her retirement in 1953 and died in
a church retirement home in Asheville, North Carolina, in
1973. Forty years' worth of her diaries and letters are in the
Sophia Smith Collection at Smith College. The prince
never came.

Many diarists had a happy marriage with their prince.
In fact, many of them conscientiously issue formal statements of their happiness — or contentment, or acceptance, or resignation — at least once a year on their
anniversaries, which the husband seldom remembers, and
they bear witness to their loss when their husbands die,
although these tender testimonies are not without their
expression of dread as well, because most widows, with
good reason, fear for their own survival. They also wonder
who they are; after years of being their children's mother

and their husband's wife, they want to find themselves. The search often becomes the primary work of the diary, conscious or not. In the early years, however, those of the so-called courtship diaries, the search is simply for love.

Women have been defined by love and define themselves by it. "Of man's life a thing apart," as Milton described it, love has been women's vested interest, based on the old, unwritten covenant: her love and life in return for his care. As such it occupies mind-time and diary-space, not only in the courtship diaries but in later diaries, too. Of course, there were marriages without love, but with or without it, marriage was defined by babies.

Contemporary and friend of the lexicographer Samuel Johnson, English gentlewoman Hester Thrale (1741–1821) met her husband once before her arranged marriage with him. In the ensuing fifteen years, not counting miscarriages, she bore him twelve children, of which eight died young. She and her husband were not in love. She writes, "We lived on terms of great civility and politeness, if not of strong alliance and connection.... As I never was a fond wife, so I certainly never was a jealous one; I soon saw that I was married from prudential motives, as a passive, though well born and educated girl...."

Her first husband gave her what may have been the first set of "nothing books" — calf-bound blank books in which to record the history of her family and perhaps her thoughts. The published record, known as *Thraliana*, is long since out of print, but the complete manuscripts may be found in the Houghton Library, Harvard University.

After her first husband's death, Hester Thrale married her daughters' Italian music master, Gabriel Piozzi, who history reports to have been a much younger man but who Thrale reports was "half a year *older* when our registers were examined." In a long, serious journal entry, she weighs the pros and cons of marrying for love and questions her situation:

> October 1, 1872
> I married the first time to please my mother, I must marry the second time to please my daughter....
> But why?

Why indeed? She continues, asking herself, "[I]s it wise to place one's happiness on the continuance of *any* man's affection?"

She married the piano teacher against the objections of her family and of her friend, Dr. Johnson. She writes later, on January 25, 1785, that her heart is "made vulnerable by my late marriage." Was the world well lost? She outlived Piozzi, too, and notes with painful irony (March 30, 1809): "Everything most dreaded *has* ensued — all is over; and my second husband's death is the last thing recorded in my first husband's present! Cruel Death!"

Which is better: a comfortable loveless marriage or an all-consuming passion? By which does a woman flourish? Love is not necessarily comfortable nor ever entirely welcome.

Sophia Tolstoy (1844-1919) at the age of eighteen had the misfortune to fall in love with and marry a moody genius twice her age, a womanizer by whom she bore thirteen children. She had no occupation to call her own, except serving as secretary and copyist of Leo Tolstoy's work, rearing their children, and managing the estates — work enough! Yet she feels trapped:

> November 13, 1862
> ... I can't find any occupation for myself. He is
> lucky to be so clever and talented. But I'm neither
> the one nor the other. One can't live on love alone.

Sophia turned to her diary for reassurance. She sees herself as a doll-wife, "not a *human being*." She blames herself for her troubles while confessing her envy of her husband's independence of her:

> November 23, 1862
> He disgusts me with his People. I feel he ought to
> choose between me, i.e. the representative of the
> family and his beloved People. This is egoism, I know.

Her fault, she thinks, not his. By January 17, 1863, she is certain the fault lies in herself: "[T]he real source of all my troubles and bad mood is my egoism and my idea that his whole life, his thoughts, and his love must belong to me."

Even in their private diaries, women have always been ready to take the blame. And even when they have nothing left to give, women feel guilty for not being able to give more. The attitude is not innate but acquired; it took centuries of training. To question it can crumble the foundations of a life. As Sophia Tolstoy writes:

September 12, 1865
I have always been told that a woman must love her
husband and be honourable and be a good wife
and mother. They write such things in ABC books,
and it is all nonsense.

And they said she was unbalanced.

The American anthropologist Ruth Fulton Benedict
(1887–1948) married biochemist Stanley Benedict in 1914,
believing she had found her vocation. "What need has a
happy woman to 'justify her existence'?" she asks her journal in her first happy year of marriage. After seven childless years, during which she fell into anthropology as if it
were meant to be, taking her Ph.D. from Columbia in two
years, she writes (undated): "I must have my world too, my
outlet, my chance to put forth my effort." She says rueful-
ly, "I haven't strength of mind not to need a career."

By October 1920, Benedict acknowledges in her journal how much she and her husband are hurting each other,
yet she realizes that

The more I control myself to his requirements, the
greater violence I shall do my own — kill them in
the end.... All he asks is to keep an even tenor. And,
knowing this, for years I can keep away from subjects which disrupt the quiet — my own ambi-
tions; my sense of futility; children — chiefly
children.... The greatest relief I know is to have put
something in words, no matter if it's as stabbing as
this is to me ... better than an utter silence about

his viewpoint, year in and year out. — And so it's insoluble —

Benedict's career was important to her as was her husband's to him; they were separated several years before his death in 1936.

Katherine Mansfield also struggled with the problem of love versus career: "It is the hopelessly insipid doctrine that love is the only thing in the world, taught, hammered into women, from generation to generation, which hampers us so cruelly. What are we going to do about it?" But she bought the fairy-tale, while still wanting something else:

> Summer, 1913
> Oh, Jack, I wish a miracle would happen — that you would take me in your arms and kiss my hands and my face and every bit of me and say "It's all right, you darling thing. I quite understand."

A good man, like a good marriage, is hard to find, though some women in every century claim to have found him, as we read of happily-ever-after anticipation in their diaries. Before and After: nothing presents a greater contrast to a woman than the delicious expectation before marriage — the hopes and dreams and fantasies of Prince Charming — and the reality after the bells stop ringing. Living happily ever after proves to be very hard work, presenting never-ending tasks, but Prince Charming or his closest equivalent still looks like the best bet, even in this century, especially if a woman wants children.

Lucy Maud Montgomery was married on July 5, 1911.

She describes her wedding in a long journal entry on January 28, 1912, after first giving voluminous attention to the death of her grandmother (March 10, 1911). Finally, she turns to her marriage, still writing in retrospect:

> The last fortnight before my marriage was an intensely busy one. There were a thousand and one things to do and every day seemed hotter than the last.
>
> Ewan came Tuesday night. The marriage was to take place next day, Wednesday, July 5th, at noon [she was thirty-seven years old in 1911]. That night I did two things I had never exactly pictured myself as doing the night before my wedding day. I cried for a little while after I went to bed — and then I slept soundly the rest of the night!
>
> I hardly know why I cried. I was not unhappy. I was quite contented. I think I wept a lost dream — a dream that could never be fulfilled — a girl's dream of the lover who should be her perfect mate, to whom she might splendidly give herself with no reservations. We all dream that dream. And when we surrender it unfulfilled we feel that something wild and sweet and unutterable has gone out of life!

She concludes, "Yes, I was content."

In previous centuries, not many women were that fortunate. Arranged and forced marriages, no-other-choice marriages, steely- as opposed to starry-eyed marriages

offered about equal chances of happiness. The only real difference lies in the woman's attitude.

Even those who have seemed to accept their lot still
break out in their diaries with a comment about husbands,
or men, or marriage in general. "Little Emmy" Gillespie,
who trembled on the eve of her marriage, became more
cynical as the years and marriage taught her hard lessons.

> April 1887
> Monday 25th: *Marriage is a lottery.* how full of
> Deceit do they come with their false tongues and
> *"there is no one as dear as thee"* until after one is mar-
> ried *then "you are mine now we have something else to
> do besides silly kissing."*

Few diarists have been so conscious of the split between
their significant other, that is, their husband, and their real
self, their diary, as was Beatrice Webb:

> October 16, 1904
> When Sydney is with me I cannot talk to the
> "Other Self" with whom I commune when I am
> alone — "it" ceases to be present and only reap-
> pears when he is absent.

Marriage did not stop Beatrice Webb from writing close
to three million words in her diaries.

German artist Paula Modersohn-Becker (1876–1907)
should probably never have married, although it seemed the
right thing to do at the time. She writes:

May 13, 1901
We are probably getting married the Saturday
before Whitsunday. Now that the time is here we
simply cannot believe it. We had gotten so used to
waiting. And now I shall be his wife.

A painter, she feels the division between her role as a wife
and her calling as an artist. Disillusion and pain do not take
long to surface:

March, 1902
In this first year of my marriage I have cried a great
deal and my tears often come like the great tears of
childhood.... When all is said and done, I'm probably just as lonely as when I was a child....

Easter Sunday, March 30, 1902
My experience tells me that marriage does not
make one happier. It takes away the illusion that
had sustained a deep belief in the possibility of
a kindred soul. In marriage one feels doubly
misunderstood.

Modersohn-Becker left her husband to paint in Paris but
she found herself caught between society's expectations of
her as wife and mother and her own fierce desire to create. Conventional standards won. She returned to her husband, bore a child, and died of an embolism eighteen days
after the birth, at the age of thirty-three. "A pity," she is
reported to have said as she died.

Anne Morrow Lindbergh (1906-1993) felt not disappointment but an enormous inevitability. The daughter of a U.S. senator, in love with the most famous man in America, shy, and terrified by the limelight, she submits to her destiny. She reports to a friend in a letter (included in her published diary, *Bring Me a Unicorn*), written shortly before her wedding to the American flying hero Charles Lindbergh:

> Apparently I am going to marry Charles Lindbergh.... Isn't it funny — why does one marry, anyway? I didn't expect or want anything like this.... But after all, what am I going to do about it? After all, there he is and I've got to go. I wish I could hurry and get it over with soon. This horrible, fantastic, absurd publicity and thousands of people telling me how lucky and happy I am.... I don't expect to be happy, but it's gotten beyond that, somehow. Wish me courage and strength and a sense of humor.
>
> I will need them all.
>
> He has vision and a sense of humor and extraordinarily nice eyes!

In spite of the tragedy of the kidnapping and murder of their first child, a victim of their fame, the Lindberghs had a happy marriage. Anne's published, best-selling diaries attest to that.

American sociologist Jessie Barnard (*The Future of Marriage*) believes that in every marriage there are two marriages: his and hers. Men consider marriage to be a trap for men and a prize for women but in actuality, his is more convenient and happier than hers. Diarists bear that out over the centuries, with their hints of resentment. Actually, the early ones hint; later ones declare: marriage for women was a hard life.

Proof of the real danger to women's well-being lies in the mortality rates of women in the century before this one. In an anthology of pioneer women's diaries, *Women of the West*, editors Cathy Luchetti and Carol Olwell reveal the statistics: "Even in the relatively 'safe' territories of Dakota, Nebraska, Utah, and Washington the death rate of women between 1859 and 1860 was 22 percent higher than that of men, including violent deaths. An 1865 study showed the mortality rates in Ohio and Illinois of women between twenty and fifty to be 50 percent higher than men's."

As late as the beginning of this century, female life expectancy in North America was only forty-eight years. Women died in childbirth: before, during, and after. If they escaped that, they died of consumption because they always received less food and less sleep and less care when they did get sick. In the west, at any rate, they died of sheer exhaustion, literally worked to death. The hardship of their lives is recorded in their diaries.

That, of course, was in pioneer times when no one had it easy. The men were working like slaves too. Poverty takes its toll on anyone. In this century, southern housewife Magnolia Le Guin, ill and tired with all her pregnancies, takes the time to comment on how hard her husband works and how tired he is.

June 14 (1903)

"Papa Ghu" works *so hard*, so hard. I wish he could live without so much *hard* labor on farm — wish he could do only such work as did not overtax him. He has worked very hard and is not well. He coughs and has a cold all the time lately. I am sorry. I am so sick myself that I can not do very much and have to lie down a great deal. God be with us.

[and late that evening, written on the same day] Ghu has been working *very* hard and has overtaxed his strength and hasn't been well lately. He is a *very hard* worker — has too much energy for his strength. I sometimes fear he will shorten [his] life by too much hard work on farm. He hurries so and does much more work than any man he has hired.

In fact, Ghu outlived Magnolia by three years.

What about the higher classes of women, the pampered ones with servants and leisure time, the ones who could read and write and leave a record of their doings? They must have been healthier than the poor ones. Some must have possessed enormous stamina and vitality to bear so many babies, usually one a year, and keep on keeping on. Even upper-class women, though, had no rights within marriage and few women, given the odds and opportunities, were able to hold out against marriage. There was still more future within than without it; without it there was less physical pain perhaps, if one didn't have a baby, but no security at all.

The American professional diarist Mary MacLane (1881-1929), born in Winnipeg and raised in Montana, made a fortune with her wits by publishing a diary so personal it became an instant best-seller. She never married, as she maintained in her diaries that she would not: "I would rather have a farthing's value as a faithful concubine than no value as a slattern housewife." Few women have dared to make that conscious choice before this century. Until quite recently the choice, admittedly, was limited: madonna or whore, maiden or hussy or governess — not much to choose from. MacLane stayed with her choice and spent the last years of her life in Chicago, where she died destitute in a hotel room at the age of forty-eight.

At least marriage held out some promise of companionship and security in one's old age, especially if a woman had one or two children to look after her. But most diaries begin and continue out of loneliness. Some may begin with a lonely little girl, orphaned or partly so, ignored or neglected, left on her own, at any rate, with few resources. She turns to paper as her friend and companion. Diaries begin after marriage as well, for much the same initial reason: loneliness, a need to communicate. Even if a woman was already a diarist, she found additional reason to write if there was some failing in her marriage. In other centuries, there was no questioning marriage or the status quo. Her safest course was to find a paper pal.

When a woman has found a companion in her husband, she usually has no need of a diary, unless she's like Beatrice Webb who had both. The Webbs' spare moments were spent together, enjoying each other's company, sharing thoughts, plans, hopes, dreams, satisfaction, troubles or fears, but especially — work.

Other might-have-been diarists were content if they had someone to tell at the end of the day how many pies they baked or how much cloth they wove — whether or not he paid attention. All he has to do, all he has ever had to do, is make sympathetic noises.

This may be considered a twentieth-century problem, the idea that *he* doesn't listen, but past diarists also report a lack of communication. Mary Richardson Walker (1811-1897), one of the first white women to cross the Rockies, tried on Friday, July 26, 1839, to break the sound barrier after a year and a half of marriage.

> To Rev. E. Walker,
> My dear Husband I find it in vain to expect my
> journal will escape your eyes & indeed why should
> I wish to have it [so]?
>
> Certainly my mind knows no sweeter solace
> than the privilege of unbosoming itself to you. It
> frequently happens that when I think of much I
> wish to say to you, you are either so much
> fatigued, so drowsy or so busy that I find no con-
> venient opportunity till what I would have said is
> forgotten. I have therefore determined to address
> my journal to you. I shall at all times address you
> with the unrestrained freedom of a fond &
> confiding wife. When therefore you have leisure

& inclination to know my heart, you may here find it ready for converse.

Husband as diary? Not likely.

Female Friendships Are Subversive

> IN FRIENDSHIP, WOMEN DO FOR EACH OTHER
> WHAT CULTURE EXPECTS THEM TO DO FOR MEN
> AND IN THAT WAY, FEMALE FRIENDSHIPS ARE
> SUBVERSIVE.
>
> *Louise Bernikow*

The descriptions of great friendships in history and literature have seldom acknowledged those between women. ("Women have no history," as Virginia Woolf once said.) Think of David and Jonathan, Jesus and John the Baptist, Arthur and Lancelot, Hamlet and Horatio, Tom Sawyer and Huck Finn. The reason for the silence about female friendship is partly, of course, that men write about male friendship and ignore female relationships except where they directly serve (or hinder) men. Then, too, few women were published on any subject from earliest times through to the mid-seventeenth century. Literate women whose writing has survived, including their diaries, do sometimes gratefully refer to the assistance and devotion of their women friends. However, their survival depended on their relationship with the men in their life, a father, usually a husband, even a missing one. If there were a man present in their lives, he was the one they owed gratitude and mind-time.

In other centuries marriage was recognized as a death blow to female friendship. American feminist writer Louise Bernikow cites seventeenth-century English poet Katherine Phillips (1632-1664) as an early proponent of friendship. Phillips took the pseudonym Orinda and formed a male and female Society of Friendship, an important Renaissance concept. Married herself (Phillips was her married name), Orinda warned of the effect of marriage on friendship; she writes in a letter that few friendships in the world are "marriage-proof." Perhaps that was truer then than now, but it has been a problem of women in past generations. One method that men have used to control women has been that of division and conquest: united we stand, divided you fall. Once women marry, it is made clear to them that their first loyalty is to husband and family. Their female friendships fall by the wayside; if they do not fall, they lose their strength and hold. Thus a woman who is staunch and true, that is, united with her family against all foes, is separated from her female friends, and therefore, in a serious way, from herself. And yet women have always needed their women friends. "There is no real happiness," wrote Mary Granville Delany in 1727, "but in a faithful friend."

Lady Anne Clifford, who had such terrible trouble with a land-grabbing husband, acknowledges in her diary the assistance of women friends. Lady Willoughby, she reports, was kind "in the midst of all my misery" (May 4, 1616) and the queen of England secretly supported her despite Lord Dorset's appeals to the king (January 1617). Other diarists of her time and later seem almost to exist in a vacuum as far as female friends are concerned, as did many heroines of early novels. Jane Austen depicted a warm friendship between Elizabeth Bennett and her sister Jane in *Pride and Prejudice*; poor Emma Woodhouse (*Emma*) had no friends. Neither did the Brontës' Jane Eyre (*Jane Eyre*), or Catherine Earnshaw (*Wuthering Heights*), or *Villette*'s heroine, Lucy Snowe. Their eyes were turned away, from themselves and from each other.

Almost until this century, women traditionally acted as midwives, healers, and layers-out of the dead, helping one another in times of crisis. These efforts were correctly perceived not as individual acts of friendship but as community service. Little personal assertion or preference could arise in an emergency when all must be done for the sake of the one in peril. Friendship as such was irrelevant — or was it? Women's support of one another in a time of crisis often goes beyond mere aid, as women can still testify today.

As more women learned to read and write, they communicated with one another on paper, like the westward-bound pioneer women who wrote their diaries faithfully in the guise of writing letters to friends and kin and who set down the details of their harsh lives in spare, succinct, and regular reports. In their letters, as Elizabeth Hampsten reports in her book *Read This Only to Yourself*, they commiserated over the deaths in their midst and gave as much practical advice as they could about homesteading, quilt-ing, cooking, and birthing, but they seldom expressed their own feelings. That was the safest way to avoid self-pity and despair. Whether writing a letter or a diary, they just gave the news: flat facts recounted without editorializing. Women's personal writing in the centuries before this one takes careful reading.

Yet the ancient images, as Louise Bernikow points out, of women talking at the village well in earlier centuries, and — in the last century in America — of women work-ing together at quilting bees, convey a sense of camaraderie that might have been a prelude to friendship. First there had to be enough time to talk — together. Perhaps it took those bees, those gatherings, to bring women together in non-threatening spaces with time to talk to one another. Certainly, some breakthrough occurred.

Overtly passionate friendships — or so they seemed — began to develop between women towards the end of the nineteenth century, particularly in New England, or maybe those are simply the best known. One thinks of the rela-tionship between Olive Chancellor and Verena Tarrant in Henry James's novel *The Bostonians*, with its hints of les-bian love, at least on Chancellor's side. Women outnum-bered men by more than 50,000 after the Civil War, and Boston had become, according to James, a "sisterhood of shoppers," a "deluge of petticoats," "a city of women, a country of women." Small wonder that women turned to women for their emotional satisfaction. The arrangement came to be known as a Boston marriage, and whether or not it was lesbian, a liaison between two women was commonplace.

Henry's invalid sister Alice had just such a rewarding relationship with her companion Katharine Loring. From her diary, here is Alice's testimony to her friend:

> January 1st, 1892
> As the ugliest things go to the making of the fairest, is it not wonderful that this unholy granite substance in my breast should be the soil propitious for the perfect flowering of Katharine's unexampled genius for friendship and devotion? The story of her watchfulness, patience and untiring resource cannot be told by my feeble pen, but all the pain and discomfort seem a slender price to pay for all the happiness and peace with which she fills my days.

Women poured out affection to each other in passionate terms in their personal encounters, in their letters, and in their diaries. Historians believe that the passionate expression of love on paper was merely a convention, in no way parallelling actual behaviour. This kind of emotional kinship was certainly not exclusive to Boston. Here is L.M. Montgomery writing about a friend, in 1891, when she was seventeen:

> Friday, July 31
> Laura came home with me to stay all night. She is here now and we are just going to have a goodnight's talk.

Saturday, Aug. 1, 1891
We had it — I rather guess! We *talked* and *talked*
and *talked*. I never met a girl I could confide in as I
can in Laura. I can tell her *everything* — the
thoughts of my very inmost soul — and she is the
same with me. We are twin spirits in every way. We
talked until 2:30. Fancy!

She sounds like Anne of Green Gables!

Two English working-class women at the turn of this
century developed a close friendship and expressed it in
their diaries and in letters to each other over a period of
twenty years. Ruth Slate (1884-1953) kept her diaries
mainly between 1897 and 1909; Eva Slawson (1882-1916)
kept hers between 1913 and 1916; their letters to each other
ran between 1903 and 1916. (All their diaries and letters
are published in *Dear Girl*, edited by Tierl Thompson.)
Although she had begun a diary in 1897 when she was thirteen, Ruth didn't meet Eva until 1902. Within the year, the
two young women were corresponding and seeking each
other's company whenever they could spare time from
their busy working lives. Ruth was a clerk in a grocery firm
in London; Eva lived in Walthamstow and worked as a legal
secretary. They recommended books to each other and
offered sympathy and encouragement through various
emotional upheavals and other commitments.

We get a clear sense of Ruth's attachment to Eva from
an early diary excerpt:

12 August, 1903
It is really wonderful to hear Eva speak, she is so

very clever and has such an impartial way of looking at things. I felt freer to speak when it was to
Eva only and we told each other of the different
doubts and fears which at times had come over us.
 I feel that it is a great honour to me to have such
a friend as Eva, for I know she is much better and
nobler than I. She has said the same of me and I
was so surprised and shall I say pleased, but I am
sure she has the nobler nature.

Eva expresses a similar devotion to Ruth in a letter:

December 1904
Thank you for your last letter, Ruth, and for telling
me about Mr Randall. At first I felt a wee bit as if I
were losing my friend but I believe that the bond
between us is too strong to be severed by any new
or even dearer friendship. Keep a place always for
me in your heart, dear Ruth, I shall be all the better
for it.

These women had a little time and they were both single,
so there was nothing to prevent the blossoming of a rich
friendship, as is evidenced in their diaries and letters. That's
a great part of the secret: being single, having time.

Katherine Mansfield had a love-hate relationship with
her faithful sometime-lover and friend, Ida Baker, whom
she refers to as L.M. in her diary and letters. Tubercular,
parted from her husband Middleton Murry while she
sought health on the Italian Riviera, short of money, dependent on Baker, a companion with whom she had little in

common intellectually, Mansfield expressed murderous hatred for her:

> 20 November, 1919
>
> Think what you [her husband] would feel if you had consumption and lived with a deadly enemy! That's one thing I shall grudge Virginia [Woolf] all her days — that she and Leonard were together. We can't be: we've got to wait our six months, but when they arc up I WILL not have L.M. near. I shall rather commit suicide. That is dead earnest. In fact, I have made up my mind that I shall commit suicide if I don't tear her up by the roots then.... I leaned over the gate today and dreamed she'd died of heart-failure and I heard myself cry out "Oh, what heaven! what heaven!"

L.M. was safe enough; a month earlier Mansfield had written, "I shall never shoot her because the body would be so difficult to dispose of after."

Two years later in Menton, near the French–Italian border, again with Ida Baker, Mansfield continues fighting as her health worsens. Yet from Paris, where she went without L.M. to seek a miraculous cure for her tuberculosis, she wrote to her contentious friend:

> 15 March, 1922
>
> *To Ida Baker* ...We cannot live together in any sense until we — I — are am stronger. It seems to me it is my job, my fault, and not yours. I am simply unworthy of friendship, as I am. I take advantage

of you — demand perfection of you — crush you — and the devil of it is that even though that is true as I write it I want to laugh. A deeper self looks at you and a deeper self in you looks back and we laugh and say "what nonsense!" It's very queer, Jones, isn't it?

One of the most famous recorded female friendships of this century grew out of a diary. Vera Brittain (1893-1970) and Winifred Holtby (1898-1935), English writers, met as students at Somerville College, Oxford, after World War One, and shared a flat in London after they graduated.

Brittain published *Testament of Youth* in 1933. Based on her diaries, the book includes the account of the deaths of Brittain's twin brother, Edward, and of her fiancé, Roland Leighton, both killed in the war. *Testament of Friendship*, subtitled "The Story of Winifred Holtby" and first published in 1940, is based on diary material as well as letters and interviews. (Brittain's actual diary, kept during World War Two and on which these books were partially based, was not actually published until after her death.) *Friendship* is not only a glowing tribute to a friend who died too young (at age thirty-seven of Bright's disease), but also, as the title implies, describes a covenant of friendship between women.

Brittain writes in a letter to Holtby, "You represent in my life the same element of tender, undistressing permanence that Edward represented, and in the end, when passion is spent and adventures are over, this is the thing that comes out on top." She is aware that sometimes a man feels threatened or subverted by his wife's female friendships. "Far from impoverishing," Brittain writes in her introduction to *Friendship*, "loyalty and affection between women is a noble relationship which ... actually enhances the love of a girl for her lover, of a wife for her husband, of a mother for her children." She says her sixteen years of unbroken friendship with Winifred taught her that "the type of friendship which reaches its apotheosis in the story of David and Jonathan is not a monopoly of the masculine sex."

In earlier times, Brittain acknowledges, this kind of friendship might have been found difficult to accept, "perhaps owing to the lack of women recorders," implying that such friendships may indeed have existed in other centuries but remained untold. In the past, men have sometimes denigrated such relationships, suggesting that such devotion between women can only be lesbian in nature. What they mean is, it's threatening; what they feel is jealousy. Children and husbands want to hear "I love you best" from the significant woman in their lives. Anything that deflects attention away from themselves is therefore suspect.

Men's friendships are different from women's. Men bond, as Lionel Tiger says; women communicate. Men fight and play with each other and drink and watch sports together; women talk with each other. Which of the activities better shares insights and clarifies self? Women have often been considered, by men, to be incapable of true friendship with other women. Certainly jealousy and envy, and competition for the male, have divided women in the past and in the past men have fostered these negative emotions in order to increase loyalty to and dependency on themselves. Without female friends, without a communicative husband, not forsaking but failing all others, only then have women turned to their diaries for their ultimate friendship.

American Quaker Deborah Norris Logan (1761–1839) had begun a journal in 1815, when she was fifty-four, and settled firmly into the habit after her husband's death in 1821. She kept up this communication with her paper friend until a few weeks before her death at seventy-eight. Herewith a few entries from her last week of recording:

January, 1839
I was alone last evening and worked industriously
at my needle. The needle is a great friend to
woman.

I am old and infirm and want kindness and
comfort, no anxiety and care, which however seems
to fall to my lot at present.

I do not look forward to much longer life.

... seated in the dining room I seem quite incapable of helping others or of being pleased myself.

I am waiting for my breakfast as are the pet
chickens for theirs. I do not feel at all pleasant or
efficient. And it is not possible to get along with
dowdy help unless you seem smart and capable
yourself.

One thing I know — I am exceedingly unwell,
my stomach is not good and my ankles are swelled

very much…. Only the sunny picture of the tree growing out of the rock on the wall pleases me. Now that is fast vanishing away. It is gone!

When all else falls away, family, friends, youth, health, love, and friendship, a woman's diary remains: *"My old journal, my friend."*

If they are silent about what went on in the heterosexual bed, diarists of other centuries are even more silent about same-sex love. Many of them probably didn't even recognize their own predilections. They were so brainwashed into believing in Prince Charming and Sleeping Beauty that it may never have occurred to them that Snow White might actually prefer Rose Red.

Mary MacLane is among the first diarists to spell it out:

Do you think a man is the only creature with whom one may fall in love?

I am someway the Lesbian woman. It is but one phase — one which slightly touches each other phase I own….

— all women have a touch of the Lesbian: an assertion all good non-analytic creatures refute with horror, but quite true: there is always the poignant intensive personal taste, the flair of inner-sex, in the tenderest friendships of women.

For myself, there is no vice in my Lesbian vein….

I don't know whether I am good and sweet in it or evil and untoward. And I don't care.

One cannot help but suspect the writer of grandstanding.

Eva Slawson was probably bisexual, if her report of an erotic physical encounter with a married woman friend is to be believed. Yet she wants marriage, a complete one, based on "a three-fold attraction — physical, mental, spiritual." She has a good friend in Minna, the married friend, and in Ruth, her long-time buddy, but she knows something is missing:

> June 19, 1913
> I realised to the full how inevitably we single women are "outside the heart of things"; our friendship with happily married men and women after all only touches the fringe of their lives.

She ponders Minna's ideas:

> September 9, 1913
> [Minna] says she thinks a man unsatisfactorily married suffers and hungers more than a woman because a woman can find comfort in the depths of another woman, but very seldom a man in another man — and sex is the barrier to prevent him finding it in another woman. Yet I believe it is possible to transcend sex.

Still thinking about marriage, she writes:

> January 22, 1914
> — it is certainly one of the great fundamentals of life, without which one is the poorer, but I think it is a morbid and unhealthy view to take that a

woman's life is a failure because she never experiences love and marriage.

Her own friendships have proved otherwise:

August 14, 1914
I do think it should be recognised there are women, as well as men, capable of the finest friendship.

"Marion Taylor" (1902-1960), a pseudonym for a young girl who was fearful from the very beginning about her diary being read, discovered later in life, after a childless marriage and divorce, that she was lesbian. She kept it a secret so as not to lose her teaching job but she lived with another woman for the last years of her life until her sudden death at the age of fifty-eight. With hindsight, can a reader interpret a few hints of Marion's future in her teenaged diary? In 1915 she was thirteen years old:

April 22
If I ever am fool enough to marry I shall marry a quite grave, serious, man; literary in his tastes and a great deal older than I.... But I do want to be an old maid! My disposition is not suited to marriage.

July 13
My Hero. If I marry which I hope I never shall do as I think I am too old maidish to get along well with a man I shall marry no younger than at twenty-five (by then I ought to have a little sense).... I will not expect any romantic ravishing love like in books. I shall never have children.

April 28, 1916
I wish that a certain person I loved, loved me one-
tenth as much as I do them. But I suppose there
isn't much in a sentimental, self-conscious, gawky,
common, ordinary little girl for a charming, witty,
wonderful woman like M.G. [one of her teachers]
to like when there's so many interesting, lovely girls
in the school.

February, 1918
One can't blame men for liking feminine women.
Young ladies are such adorable things. If I were a
man I'd make love to them all.

Contemporary diarists, of course, still remain to be heard
from. Among the excerpts available in collections, I sense
a new openness among women, a greater interdependence,
and a purer appreciation of their value as friends. American
diarist Sonny Wainwright, for example, battling cancer,
reports a celebration with her female friends:

June 4, 1983
The unpredictable Janet gave me a party, and we
invited all the women who have been involved: all
my supporters for this first half of my treatment
program.... It was a wonderful blend of women
who have touched my life in different ways!

American poet Kathleen Spivack offers a small bouquet of
disparate diary entries in *Ariadne's Thread*, a collection of
contemporary women's journals gathered by Lyn Lifshin.

Two of them suggest the firmer, accustomed place friends now hold in women's lives and the lesser dependency on men:

> October 1979
> Barb here, Manya, friends from all over. Marilyn. Men going in and out of our lives. Feeling of peace, completeness. If this is all there is, it will just have to be all right.

A woman's subterranean life keeps flowing, her subconscious secure, as she continues to care for her family and friends, in a true laying-on of hands. The hands, however, still reach for a diary, a friend in need.

Let Them Break Quietly

> WOMEN ARE INTENDED FOR TWO THINGS: TO BRING CHILDREN INTO THE WORLD AND TO MAKE MEN COMFORTABLE, AND THEN THEY MUST KEEP QUIET AND IF THEIR HEARTS BREAK WITH GRIEF, LET THEM BREAK QUIETLY — THAT'S ALL.
>
> *Nellie McClung*

Grief was often the first lifeline uttered in a diary. In other centuries when both reticence and lack of paper limited expression, pain broke through the constraints, demanding recognition. In bereavement the chief pain of the loss comes from the loss of self. An investment has been made in the loved one: spouse, child, parent, friend. The closer the love has been, the deeper the emotional investment. In order to survive and continue with one's own life, one has to withdraw the self that was entrusted to the other person. This is what grieving is all about. Whatever the cause of the emotional wound, the recovery has to start within the consciousness of the person suffering. When the internal pain becomes unbearable, it may burst onto the private pages of a diary.

This cry is probably the first encounter an early diarist has with an unacknowledged self, as she struggles to recover, to pull herself out of pain, to reassure herself that she will survive. She begins to sense the inner self that has to be reached, touched, healed. She probably begins to be aware of the distance between her inner and outer selves and of the necessity to close the gap.

Although contemporary women are encouraged to record their grief or their trauma, whether bereaved or abused, they must always have known the benefits of this instinctively. In private pages without fear of criticism or false cheer, a woman can examine her reactions, no matter how inconsistent or irrelevant: shock, despair, denial, comfort, tears, despair, pain, anger, depression, despair, hope, fear, guilt, self-pity, despair. A diarist can go through all the stages of grief as many times as she needs to. Grief is a staggering experience but it can be an immensely creative process, a learning, growing evolution. Whether keeping household accounts or reporting their spiritual or physical progress, women in the past found that an instrument was in place — paper — just when they needed it.

One of the first women on record to give vent to her grief by this means was Marguerite Mercier. According to *A History of Private Life*, a rare journal reveals that this early seventeenth-century Parisian bourgeoise kept the household accounts book for her husband. Mercier reported the birth of "our child," a little girl, in the accounts book, because the family purchased baby equipment: a wicker cradle and cloth for it, a basket, cover, mattress. The child, referred to as "*la petite*" ("the little girl"), was sent out to a wet nurse, whose salary was noted. Other entries followed: shoes, stockings, gloves, a child's chair, toys. The little girl was almost two when she came home and her name, Nanette, entered the accounts. But Nanette got sick, a doctor was called, she was bled. More shoes and stockings; was she better? Silence.

Mercier "forgot to write" three times during this period. In a shaky hand, she confesses these omissions that her historian notes never occurred before or after. Then she lists another expense, a single line: "6 l.[livres] to bury my poor child." *Poor child* is the understatement of an emotion wrenched into recognition.

With literacy, it became possible to communicate distress, albeit quietly, privately, by setting it down on paper. Thus a personal act of communication occurs, one that does not require an audience of more than one for the event to have been acknowledged. Later readers must infer the pain it records, not by what is actually written, but by the fact that it is written at all.

It has been my observation that people change, if ever,

after a shock. The death of her life companion, and to a somewhat lesser extent, parent or child, throws a diarist's life and perceptions into sharp relief: Before and After. *That was then, this is now.*

The story is old and timeless. I offer a quilt of precious scraps, culled from three centuries of pain. The names of some of the women are familiar; most are not. The common denominator here is grief, through the centuries.

Alice Thornton (1668)

Great are my calamities; my case is full of complaints, bereft of a most dear and tenderly loving husband that took part with me in all sorrows, comforted me in sadnesses. We walked together as dear friends. His love was mine, in his sickness I was afflicted. Now am I left of him who was my earthly delight, he being gone to his heavenly father and left me to lament his loss from me and my poor fatherless children, weak in body, afflicted in spirit, low in my estate [meaning status as well as money].

Hannah Allen (1683)

After I heard of the death of my husband (for he died beyond sea) I began to fall into deep melancholy. And no sooner did this black humour begin to darken my soul, but the Devil set on with his former temptations, which at first were with less violence and frequent intermissions, but yet with great strugglings and fightings within me. As I would express it to my aunt, "I am just as if two were fighting within me, but I trust the Devil will never be able to overcome me."

Thus began the account of a very long depression.

Mary Shelley (1815)

March 6

Find my baby dead. Send for Hogg. Talk. A miserable day.

March 7

Not in good spirits. Hogg goes at 11. A fuss. To bed at 3.

March 9

Read and talk. Still think about my little baby. 'Tis hard, indeed, for a mother to lose a child.

March 13

Shelley and Clara go to town. Stay at home ... and think of my little dead baby. This is foolish, I suppose; yet, whenever I am left alone to my own thoughts, and do not read to divert them, they always come back to the same point — that I was a mother, and am so no longer.

Mrs. William W. Todd (1818)

I am now a Widow, I have no bosom friend to go to in seasons of perplexity for advice, no one with whom I can unreservedly share all my griefs and Sorrows, all my Joys and pleasures.... I did love him, alas but too tenderly — we lived together on such terms as man and wife ought to live, placing perfect confidence in each other, bearing one another's burdens and making due allowances for human imperfections.

Sarah Ripley Stearns (1848)
Rain all day. This day my dear husband, my last remaining friend, died.... Today we buried my earthly companion. Now I know what none but widows know; that is, how comfortless is that of a widow's life, especially when left in a strange land, without money or friends, and the care of seven children.

Linka Keyser (1854)
It is exactly a year ago today since sister Waleska died — the beloved sister! — I think of thee very often, and frequently talk with thee. But that conversation is so strange and I wonder why? No doubt I am too earthbound to commune with thee who already art with God in heaven. My thoughts seem always to revolve about things transitory. When the dear memories of the days we spent together rise up before me, I still remain earthbound.

Mary Richardson Walker (1877)
I feel so lonely. [I] think of so many things to want to tell Mr. Walker. I realize more and more how much more I loved him than any one else.

Gretel Lainer (c. 1912)

Mama died on the 24th of April, the Sunday after
Easter.... Why do people have to die? Or at least it
should only be quite old people, whom no one
cares about any more. But a mother and a father
ought never to die.

Frances Gunther (1949)

Missing him now, I am haunted by my own short-
comings, how often I failed him. I think every parent must have a sense of failure, even of sin, merely
in remaining alive after the death of a child. One
feels that it is not right to live when one's child has
died, that one should somehow have found the way
to give one's life to save his life.

Anne Philipe (1959)

[addressing her dead husband] How is it possible
that I live — not that I live, but simply that my
heart continued to beat now that yours has
stopped? ... I still find it difficult to live in the
present.

Anne Truitt (1982)

I continue to grieve for James [her divorced hus-
band]. His suicide looms like a great scarped [*sic*]
rock in a desert, pitted and fissured, cutting off the
horizon of his life.... When I mourn, I do mourn
what he and I never had: the lovely entire confidence that comes only from innumerable mutual
confidences entrusted and examined.... I mourn

because I am now living alone in the light of these insights. The clasped hands of old couples make me sad.

Le Anne Schreiber (1987)
Last night I dreamt that my mother appeared to me when I was sad.... This morning, I still feel good about the dream, even though it did not have an aura about it the way certain, very significant dreams do. It's the best image I've had so far, and I'll take it, thank you.

M.T. Dohaney (1989)
I'm beginning to accept your death — or accept the fact of your death. I no longer get jolted by the unrumpled pillow and I no longer look for your car in the driveway when I come home from work. But there are aspects I can't accept. Will you never again rub your beard over my cheek, hug my body, ruffle my hair, hold my hand or warm my feet?

Through her grief-writing, this last widowed author finally comes to terms with what she gained as well as with what she lost. Her gradual relief accompanies the assertion of self, a sure sign of recovery:

I want to thank you for who I am. Without you, I never would have gone to university, written a novel or learned to play cribbage. I also want to thank you for fostering my self-confidence. And I forgive you for dying — at least I do at this moment. Tomorrow I may be back to "How could you do such a dastardly deed to me?"

Before the night is over I might even drum up enough magnanimity to thank God for loaning you to me. It was such a quality loan.

In other centuries, when they scarcely knew how to identify their emotions, let alone express them, women found an outlet in their diaries. Whatever shorthand they used, whatever code, whatever was buried in litany or euphemism or silence, these diarists wrote down what they could. The words they wrote and the lines we read bear rereading. Any major life event that shakes the foundations of one's comfortable assumptions and rooted beliefs triggers an explosion of emotion, and then an eruption of questions: Who am I now? What am I doing here? Where am I going?

These questions keep popping up. With hindsight forced and clarified by shock, a diarist can look back and see where she's coming from and, without invalidating her past, she can rise like Persephone from the darkness. A diary provides a refuge where she can rage, scream, cry, tear out her figurative hair, rant, rave, wallow in self-pity, go mad, threaten God — and no one has to know. The face presented to the public remains serene. Some people tear up their incendiary pages, or burn them. Others keep them as records of the depths or heights to which they have fallen or aspired.

Today, a daily journal offers space and time for a full range of emotions, so that the writer need not be limited, except by her own blocks and choices, which admittedly can be as restrictive as material, physical restraints were in centuries past. First, however, one has to acknowledge the emotion before one can recognize it. American psychologist Jean Baker Miller says that women have been so "encouraged to concentrate on the emotions and reactions of others that they have been diverted from examining and expressing their own emotions." In diaries women get that chance, even in other centuries when they scarcely knew how to identify their emotions, let alone examine them, and when a terrible reticence held the writer back from her full expression. Putting words to feelings provides some comfort and leaves a few lifelines, however slender, for those who follow.

CHAPTER THREE

Life Is So Daily

WOMEN'S JOURNALS PERFORCE RECORD
MORE DOMESTIC DETAILS THAN MEN'S —
POSSIBLY THIS IS WHY THEY ALSO SEEM
MORE INTERESTING, CERTAINLY MORE
PERTINENT.

Maxine Kumin

Certainly the domestic details of a woman's life are more interesting and pertinent — to a woman — than the external events of the world at large. To be a woman diarist is to maintain a balance between your outer and your inner life, creating your own allotted space wherein you are not obligated but are free to watch yourself, moving around within the boundaries of your life, discovering with the eye of an observer what that life is like. I spy — me with a spoon, me with a trowel, dishcloth, diaper, fan, usually confined to the house and garden in the centuries before this one. Even today, women seldom write about world events as they live through them. They focus instead on the minutiae of daily life and on relationships within the family and community. Perhaps their emphasis over the centuries has been a matter of necessity: an attempt to establish one's sense of self in the larger world in an easy, non-threatening way.

Here I am, ten, twenty, forty-two years old, and there you are, my mother, my husband, my child, my home, my daily work. This is what I am about. This is who I am.

A Prize or a Blank

> WE FIND IT REITERATED, OF COURSE, WITH EMPHASIS, THAT TO MARRY, AND TO MARRY WELL, IS THE ONE GREAT OBJECT OF YOUNG GIRLS' ENERGIES AND DESIRES. ACCORDING AS A GIRL MARRIES OR NOT, LIFE IS A PRIZE OR A BLANK.
>
> *Henry James*

As we have seen, a terrible reticence falls on women of earlier times when it comes to discussing their bodily functions, even to themselves. Menstruation and menopause, sexual intercourse, birth control, parturition, masturbation, and the expression of same-sex love — all have been either ignored completely or obliquely glossed over in the most private of diaries, a fact that more tellingly than any other confirms the idea that diarists have always been uncomfortably aware of a possible audience, intended or not. The same discretion usually extends to the services performed in connection with these life events, specifically, midwifery and appropriate assistance to the dying and dead — the laying-on of hands. What most diarists lack in explicitness about sex, however, they make up for in their often fulsome attention to death.

Contemporary grandmothers are astonished at their tiniest granddaughters' accuracy in identifying their private parts by name, the more so because, as enlightened as this generation is, it failed to teach its daughters. Earlier mothers, especially the Victorian ones, didn't even warn their daughters about menstruation, let alone sex. Anything to do with the human body, anything sexual, was swathed in secrecy. To be ignorant was to be innocent, or so they thought. The result, of course, was far from innocence. The result was insatiable curiosity, persistent fixation, indefatigable experimentation, and accidents. If you didn't know what caused babies, what could you do to avoid them, or even space them?

Emily Gillespie must have found a method of birth control, for she bore only three children, one of them a twin who died at birth, while her neighbours and sister kept on having babies. She went to visit a friend, Lizzie, in Masonville, and reports.

October 1873. Thursday 2.
Lizzie has two boys (twins) 5 mos. old. O dear, I think she has her hands full & heart, too, five children (one little boy died a year ago) — all so young — why, the oldest is only seven years old the 10th of last month, how thankful I am that I am not in such circumstances it seems I could not endure so much trouble, Aye, the old saying is but

too true, — "those capable of enduring most have most to bear."

Emily's sister Harriet had babies with dismaying regularity, a fact that Emily reports with smug pity. "*Enceinta* again," she writes. In March 1882, Emily reports a miscarriage:

Sun 19
I went to see Harriet, she looks very bad indeed. I
am really sorry for her. Ah me! such is the life of
most women.

Perhaps Gillespie's method of birth control was simply abstinence, which could account for her husband James's growing coldness and anger towards her. Her own increasing unhappiness emerges as well:

August 1874
'tis now three o'clock & here I am writing once
more in my journal, the only confidant I ever had,
& thou dear journal dost not know every secret.
nay! nay!

The most explicit description of what might be what she calls "the secret to be burried" comes on March 25, 1883:

James is at the barn, he went without his supper
because of a very unpleasant time we had — tis too
bad — but I can not always endure everything. he
would turn us all out of doors if he could. (when a
man lays his hands hold of his wife & Children I
think tis time something was done)

On the other hand, the secret could have been something that happened before her marriage. She includes a very strange poem, obviously addressed to someone other than her husband, hinting at a previous love. Gillespie isn't saying.

Circumspect as she is, she does comment in her diary on her daughter's first period:

> February 1880 Sun 29
> Sarah not very well. (Menses first.)

Sarah was fifteen years old.

A few younger diarists have commented on their menarche, Jewish teenager Anne Frank among them:

> Wednesday, 5 January, 1944
> I think what is happening to me is so wonderful,
> and not only what can be seen on my body, but all
> that is taking place inside. I never discuss myself or
> any of these things with anybody; that is why I
> have to talk to myself about them.
> Each time I have a period — and that has only
> been three times — I have the feeling that in spite
> of all the pain, unpleasantness, and nastiness, I have
> a sweet secret, and that is why, although it is noth-
> ing but a nuisance to me in a way, I always long
> for the time that I shall feel that secret within
> me again.

Alice is the pseudonym for an anonymous American teenager who died of an accidental overdose of drugs in the sixties. She kept a diary of her experiences as a runaway and at home when she returned in an attempt to clean up her act. In a hopeful, quiet moment, she takes time to make a rare comment about herself and her body:

> April 14
> I got up really early this morning so I could take a long leisurely bath.... After I shaved my legs and underarms, I really looked at my body critically for the first time in my life. Its a nice body.... I'm glad I'm a girl. I even like having my periods.

Funnily, though she is not a virgin, she fears using a tampon instead of a sanitary napkin in case she upsets her mother.

Evelyn Lau (b. 1970) is a young Chinese-Canadian honour-roll student who took to the streets, drugs, and sex at the age of fourteen rather than live with her restrictive parents. She is as explicit about her periods as she is about everything else to do with her body.

> April 6, 1986
> Pissing into a styrofoam cup for a urine sample: dark red, it's that time of month again. They have pads here [she's in a PAU — Psychiatric Assessment Unit], long and impossibly narrow, held up the old way, with belts. It's the second day of my period, and under these circumstances I have to sit tight — they don't allow underwear — afraid a sudden angry streak of scarlet will explode onto the light fabric of the hospital trousers.

What a far cry from the careful euphemisms of earlier centuries!

The sweetest one is Gretel Lainer. The mysterious teenager from pre-war Europe treats her first period as a major, exciting event:

July 2nd, perhaps about 1912
My goodness, today I have ... no, I can't write it plain out. In the middle of physics class, during revision, when I wasn't thinking of anything in particular, Fraulein N. came in with a paper to be signed. As we all stood up I thought to myself: Hullo, what's that? And then it suddenly occurred to me: Aha!! In the break Hella [her closest friend] asked me why I had suddenly gone bright red in physics class, if I'd had some sweets with me.... I said: "Oh no...."

On the way home I was very silent and walked so slowly (for of course one mustn't walk fast when ...) that Hella said: "Look here, what has happened today to make you so frightfully solemn? Have you fallen in love without my knowing it, or is it at long last...?" then I said "Or is it at long last!" And she said: "Ah, then now we're equals again," and there in the middle of the street she gave me a kiss. ... [She worries about buying the equipment and has another thought:] it would be awful for Papa to know about it. I wonder whether men really do know; about their wives, perhaps, but certainly not about their daughters.

English novelist Virginia Woolf was acutely aware of the effect on her creativity of what she called her "flux." When she was working on her novel *Orlando* she regrets the interruption:

> Sunday, February 18th, 1928
> I had thought to write the quickest most brilliant pages in Orlando yesterday — not a drop came, all forsooth, for the usual physical reasons, which declared themselves today. It is the oddest feeling: as if a finger stopped the flow of the ideas in the brain; it is unsealed and the blood rushed all over the place.

It's harder to find older women who mention menopause, let alone celebrate it. In other centuries, of course, few enough survived the child-bearing years to be alive to revel in the release that menopause would mean to them — and then they had to be literate as well. However, we find that voluble Hester Thrale had something to say about it:

> April 9, 1791
> I believe my oldest Friend is at last going to leave me, & that will probably make a Change in my Health, if not induce the Loss of it for ever, an odd thing has been observable on the Occasion, & merits Notice. [She describes a "Measle-Mark" which disappeared with menstruation and has now returned] ... I am now exactly 50 Years old I think, & possessed of great Corporal Strength blessed by God, with ability to endure Fatigue if necessary.

Thus she reassures herself: menopause is not the end of her world.

In this century, American anthropologist Margaret Mead (1901-1972) tried to dispel the fear women have of menopause, reassuring them of healthy, strong years ahead. Many male doctors, on the other hand, still tend to think of it as something to be "treated," perpetuating the idea that menopause is a disease. The first positive contemporary reports have appeared, including one by feminist Germaine Greer (*The Change: Women, Aging and the Menopause*). Perhaps as more diaries are written by older women, or as more come to light, we'll find out how today's women feel about the change of life.

Other silences in diaries leave great gaps of information and commentary we would welcome today. Women diarists of whatever class or century have generally been very quiet about what goes on between them and their menfolk. Explicit statements about sex cannot be found in women's diaries before this century, and not that often in this one. This silence was imposed not only from a sense of propriety but also by selection. Daily and thoughtless as a diary may seem, the diarist nevertheless chooses what to set down.

An addicted diary-reader must learn to watch for the circumlocutions, the omissions, the avoidances, the diarist's private code, and the silences. We learn as much from what people don't say as from what they do. We learn to watch for deflected communication and — if not to break the code — at least to guess at the unspoken language, and always to look for the metaphor. We must notice when people, that is, a man and a woman, have an opportunity to be alone and for how long, to decide what the diarist really means when she says they *talked*, and how far they went if she reports a kiss.

Beatrice Potter has a coy way to refer to that kind of thing. She and her fiancé, Sydney Webb, were working together on a project but it wasn't all work.

> August 11, 1891
> We allowed half an hour for talk and "human
> nature" and then worked hard at the Iron
> Founders' records. Then lunch, cigarettes, a little
> more "human nature" and then another two
> hours' work.

On August 19, she reports, "[E]vening after evening working away together undermining the individualism of the British race, with intervals of 'human nature'!"

When the pair go out of town to work and stop at a hotel (separate hotels) Potter is sure they've fooled everyone.

> October 10
> The queer little knot of the inhabitants of the hotel
> are so impressed with the bulk of my correspon-
> dence and the long hours of work that I do not
> think that they suspect the intervals of "human
> nature," but think no doubt that I keep my amanu-
> ensis hard at it all hours of the day!

Glimpses of pre-marital sex emerge in the letters and

diaries of the New World, and in reports of how children that resulted from it were cared for. New England midwife Martha Ballard describes her witness-taking: when she delivered a single mother of her child she had to inquire the father's name. It was assumed that a woman at such a time would not lie. The man, whether married or not, was then responsible for the financial care of the child. As it happens, one of her clearest reports hits close to home (errors hers):

> October 23, 1791
> Shee was safe delivered at 1 hour pm of a fine son,
> her illness very severe but I left her cleverly &
> returned ... about sun sett. Sally declard that my son
> Jonathan was the father of her child.

Jonathan later married Sally and they had several more children.

Few women in the past give us any hint in their diaries of their sex drive, with the exception of Margaret Fountaine, and, surprisingly, Queen Victoria (1819-1901).

Victoria loved Albert and sex, not necessarily in that order. They were married on February 10, 1840. Here is the blushing bride on February 11:

> When day dawned (for we did not sleep much) and
> I beheld that beautiful angelic face by my side, it
> was more than I can express. He does look so beau-
> tiful in his shirt only, with his beautiful throat seen.
> We got up at 1/4 p. 8. When I had laced I went to
> dearest Albert's room, and we breakfasted together.

He had a black velvet jacket on, without any neck-
cloth on, and looked more beautiful than it is possible for me to say....

By February 13 the happy couple were playing with each
other: "My dearest Albert put on my stockings for me. I
went in and saw him shave; a great delight for me."

American psychologist Phyllis Chesler (b. 1940), in her
wonderful diary kept during her pregnancy and the first
year after the birth of her son Aaron, surprises herself and
us with her sudden, raging desire:

> August 14, 1977
> I want to have orgasms without foreplay three or
> four times every day. I look at your father slyly, pas-
> sively.... I am without shame. Never have I been in
> such sexual heat. Is this natural in pregnancy?

Few diarists prize their bodies, let alone themselves. Mary
MacLane, the little upstart from Montana, was an exception. Her first edited diary, *The Story of Mary MacLane*, was
published in 1901, when she was twenty, and sold 80,000
copies in the first month. She was an overnight sensation.
A second book, evidently not a diary, did not do as well
and MacLane returned from the scenes of her eastern success (Chicago and New York, where she was lionized) to
Montana, to write another diary.

I, Mary MacLane again shocked and fascinated her readers and the author made a film in Chicago from a script
she had written. That was the end of her notoriety and
good fortune. While she was happy, she was outspoken:

I am rare — I am in some ways exquisite.

I so *love* my Body as it lives and breathes and moves about, with me and close to me. It is my so constant companion. It is an attractive girl, a human being of some charm.

I love my body for its woman-complexities of sex.

I am a fascinating creature.

My round white breasts beneath their black serge are concurrent with nothing settled or subservient or discreet.

If women have been discreet about describing their duties and tasks regarding sex and childbirth, they are not so about death and dying. They note and report with precise detail the last days, hours, and minutes of a family member's death and the care involved.

For centuries before this one, women played an important role in death. They nursed the sick and assisted the dying out of this life; they were responsible for the laying-out of the body. This final task of women has been taken over by professional undertakers. Earlier diarists are not silent about death in their midst. Even the most laconic accounts allow some emotion to creep into the pages when a baby dies. When the death of a parent is preceded by a terminal illness, words are more abundant, or at least acknowledge sorrow more openly. If this surprises anyone in this century, when the death of a child is considered the worst tragedy and "against nature," let it be remembered how precarious life for an infant was in the days before antisepsis and antibiotics. Bonding with a child was often steadfastly delayed until there was some assurance that the child would live. Such a delay served somewhat to deflect pain. But the loss of a parent, it seems, was a different matter. A child, even an adult one, could, and often did, indulge herself in honest emotion.

American author Louisa May Alcott describes her mother's final days with an economy of moving detail. Ill herself and unable to do much for her mother, Alcott reports in her diary for November 1877:

[I] ... pulled through, and got up slowly to help her die. A strange month....

Still feeble, and Mother failing fast. On the 14th we were both moved [at her mother's wish]....

A week in the new home, and then she ceased to care for anything. Kept her bed for three days, lying down after weeks in a chair, and on the 25th at dusk, that rainy Sunday, fell quietly asleep in my arms.

She was very happy all day, thinking herself a girl again, with parents and sisters round her. Said her Sunday hymn to me, whom she called "Mother," and smiled at us, saying "A smile is as good as a prayer." Looked often at the little picture of May [granddaughter] and waved her hand to it, "Good-by, little May, good-by!"

Her last words to Father were, "You are laying a very soft pillow for me to go to sleep on."

We feared great suffering, but she was spared

that, and slipped peacefully away. I was so glad
when the last weary breath was drawn, and silence
came, with its rest and peace.

Alcott goes on to describe the burial arrangements and
memorial service — "as she would have liked it" — and
concludes: "My duty is done, and now I shall be glad to
follow her." In fact, she lived for another eight years, but
her task was completed.

Almost everyone, sooner or later, gives a nod to God,
because that bell is going to toll for thee any time now,
make no mistake. They all knew that, these diarists, so they
cross their fingers whenever they make their plans, as, for
example, southern housewife Magnolia Le Guin: "How
uncertain is life. Lord help us to so number our days that
we may apply our hearts unto wisdom and live always
ready. Buddie [her brother] is gone from this world to
another!"

"Perhaps blood will have the freedom of the city," writes
French critic Luce Irigaray, "and the right to circulate, only
if it takes the form of ink." She could have been talking
about women's journals. Diarists may pray to have the cup
of blood pass from them; however, they know the only way
out is through. Women have always been more closely
involved with the blood sacrifice and understood its meaning better, because of the menses and also because of the
genuine hazards of childbirth. Although death from any
cause was a closer companion in other centuries than now,
it's still a possibility, and of course a certainty for everyone
in the end. When women diarists write of birth and death

and the laying-on of hands, they leave their signatures in blood. As a vivid personal statement, it's very hard to wash away.

Yet women of an earlier time were not introspective about the crises in their lives. With death, as with sex, diarists showed the effects of society's training and brainwashing. They invoked God's assistance, thanked Him for His blessings, and bowed to His will, all as part of their daily tasks. In the meantime, there was work to be done.

Variety Enough

> I AM EMPLOYED THIS DAY IN WASHING, IRONING, MENDING, DOING HOUSEWORK, READING, WRITING AND KNITTING. VARIETY ENOUGH FOR THE MOST WHIMSICAL WOMAN.
>
> *Ann Bryant Smith*

Many early diaries seem to be nothing more than the simple "telling of tasks." Scanned superficially, diaries written before the turn of this century — more specifically, the diaries of the New World, involving a different class of women — do seem to be merely that. But there are several aspects to notice about both the tasks and the telling.

First, in North America, we have to recognize to what extent women were part of a shared economy with men. Whether it was serving as the midwife in the community, as Martha Ballard did, or raising turkeys, as Emily Gillespie did for extra money for her children's education, or making cloth or cream and selling it, women's work was separate and prized, and contributed substantially to the family economy.

Thus, one of the first reasons for the telling of tasks was an economic one, to keep the accounts and to keep the records straight. Women reported their spinning, weaving, and sewing, often being paid by others for this work. In order to log what they had done and to see in writing what they had to show for their time and energy, they used journals — more like account books. The telling of tasks for many was thus a matter of accounting for their time.

The work ethic still has us by the throat. Then, as now, goal-oriented achievers, spurred by the work ethic, sought to justify their existence each day by getting as much done as possible, working as hard as they could. So it was with many of these women. The telling of the task justified the time spent, validated the day. The very repetition was satisfying: *see, see, how hard I worked!*

Another western pioneer woman reduces her days' tasks to a few words:

Tuesday, August 25, 1846
Mending, mending, day after day, stitch, stitch.

This is not to reduce a life of service to mere stitching. There was more to Maine-born Mary Richardson Walker than that. She applied for a mission to the American Board of Commissioners for Foreign Missions but was refused because she wasn't married. After an arranged meeting and brief courtship, she married a minister, Elkanah Walker, in

March 1838. Together they crossed the Rockies while Mary was pregnant, travelling by horse nearly 2,000 miles from Westport, Missouri, to Waiilatpu, Oregon, spending 129 days in all on the trail. Another missionary family, the Whitmans, were in the only existing cabin so they had to stay with them until they could build a place for themselves and their son, born December 7, 1838. They settled in Tshimakain, Oregon, but they left nine years later after the Whitmans were massacred. They moved to Willamette Valley, and in 1853, when the American Board closed operations, the couple settled in Forest Grove to raise their eight children. It was a life of relentless work:

> November 22, 1840
> I find it almost as much as I can do to take care of the children, milk, tend my fire &c from 6 o'clock in the morning till 7 at night. When I find so much that needs to be done, I can spare very little time to sleep. For several weeks I scarcely retired earlier than eleven & frequently sit up till 12 or one. I sometimes feel almost out of patience & discouraged not to say tired.

A Salisbury, New Hampshire, woman, Maria M. Fifield (1800–1861), whose diary from 1860 to 1861 has survived, demonstrates a similar economy of words to Walker's stitching testimony in an account from March 1860:

> Mon. 7th At home sewing on patchwork.
> Thurs. 8th "   "   "   "   "
> Fri. 9th   "   "   "   "   " [ditto marks hers]

The work justifies the existence of all the spinner-weaver-quilter-seamstress-diarists and gives meaning to their days. We know that and we know it more than by the mere act of their writing down the activity of each day. We know it from later entries on the same day or from comments the following year on that day's activity. Herein lies an extra reward for the diligent recorder of her diligence: the opportunity to see herself in retrospect.

Women tend to be relentlessly chronological in their thinking, as men who forget birthdays or anniversaries will be the first to acknowledge. Women constantly run a check: this day or time last year, last month, five years ago, yesterday ... I was married, gave birth, left Ohio, preserved thirty quarts of berries, wove my cloth, said farewell forever. Remembering a birth, an anniversary, a departure, or a death confirms the diarist's place in history, personal history as it is, and asserts her right to acknowledge or remember emotion. Rereading the tasks performed provides another kind of validation: that the diarist is a useful, contributing human being, that she has achieved something. She confirms her work and her time, not once but repeatedly, first in the act, then in the writing, then in the reading and rereading.

This is what I did. See what I did. I did that.

Women's work is never done, as Martha Ballard recognized: "A womans work is never Done as the Song says and happy shee whos strength holds out to the End of the rais." So much of it disappears, which is why it's never done.

Nothing lasts; all is to do again. As one old woman said, it "perishes with the usin'." No forests are forever felled or fields forever flagged with grain, but that's too poetic; the fields have to be sowed year after year. Fences, however, and buildings last a little longer than quilts and preserves. There's never anything tangible or lasting to show for women's work. A room, tidied and cleaned; a floor, swept and scrubbed; clothes, sewed, washed, and mended; food, cooked, consumed, and cleared away — all are tasks to be done again, and soon, and no one to notice unless the services are missing for too long.

As diarist Anne Langton (1794-1860) commented when everyone in her small pioneer community in Canada got sick:

> Saturday, September 19, 1846
> Now the last woman about the place is on the sick
> list, and it is much more difficult to let woman's
> work stand still than men's work. John [her brother]
> had made up his mind that nothing could be done
> on the farm, but no bread! no butter! no clean
> clothes! — this is another matter.

If not women, then at least women's work, must be replaced.

An English gentlewoman, Anne Langton emigrated to Canada with her mother and father and aunt to help her pioneering bachelor brother get settled in the Bobcaygeon area of Ontario. Her letters-cum-diaries home are full of the hazards (cold, mosquitoes) and hard work (baking, boiling soap, washing, keeping warm). As she indicates in her comment on the necessity of women's work, she was aware of how useful she was. She comes to the "firm conviction" of the importance of women and the worth of women's work and she prizes herself. She concludes, "I have ever congratulated myself that though I might be an old maid I never could be an old bachelor."

At the very least, the telling of the task completed gives some recognition and value to the work itself and to the worker who completed it. Later when she rereads her tired pages, and later still, when we read them, we discover with the diarist the validation of her existence.

This is/was I, this is me in action.

By telling herself what she has done with her time and energy, she tells herself who she is, what she is about, and why she is here. Her spinning or weaving or quilting or cooking is like Everest and her reports like Hillary's and her reason for doing what she does is the same: *because it is there.*

American psychologist Jean Baker Miller has stated the obvious when she refers to the tasks that those she calls "the dominants" don't want to perform for themselves, like doing the washing. Commercial laundromats have changed the representation of the sexes doing laundry — in public, at any rate — and men do a little more laundry in the home than they ever used to. But what a chore it must have been in the days before running hot water and automatic washers and dryers! Hard enough in the summer, but monumental and even hazardous in the winter. A number of pioneering diarists give the task some mind-time, including the above-mentioned Anne Langton, who comments with some awe on the soap-boiling she must do if there's to be any washing:

> April 6, 1846
> Soap-boiling approaches nearer to creating than anything I know. You put into your pot the veriest dirt and rubbish, and take out the most useful article.

Most diarists hate washing. Considering the time and energy the washing took, we cannot be surprised that it occupies space in early diaries. Depending on their help, the weather, and their mood, diarists had different attitudes to this chore.

A month-long chatty scrap of diary by a Nevada housewife called Rachel Haskell (n.d.) reveals her feelings in 1867:

> Thursday 28th March
> Disturbed Mr H by preparing for washing and weekly business being repugnant to his nerves. Swept rooms first and got thro well enough with the Herculean task which women all dread, but which is diversion to me, and proceeded to getting supper. [They had oyster soup — yes, in Nevada; Mr. H. ate his with vinegar.]

By the next washday, Thursday, April 21, Haskell was in a different mood:

Swept and dusted house prior to beginning the great domestic dread of the household: washing. Made bread and washed, back ached thought I should not attempt to do this another week but suppose when the day comes shall do so rather than send clothes up to town.

At least in those days washday came only once a month. In her book about housework, contemporary Canadian writer Penney Kome comments that "the woman who hauled water for her laundry probably washed once a month, rather than three times weekly, as is usual in many households now." No matter when, *Somebody Has to Do It* (the title of her book).

Another American pioneer Lizzie Wilson Goodenough (1844–?) is another confirmed diarist who knew what she'd rather be doing on Monday, July 7, 1867:

Is not this a lovely morning? It is not quite light yet, wish that my washing was done and I had nothing to do but sit here and write or enjoy myself any other way I chose, but not so, I have to go to the tub instead of the writing desk.

Mary Dodge Woodward (1826–1890) makes a discovery on a winter washday in Dakota Territory:

December 8, 1886
There is more snow than at any time last winter....
Katie [her daughter] and I have done a two weeks'
washing, hanging our clothes in the new chamber

[the family was building an addition to the house]
which is a capital place. Everybody in Dakota
should have a covered place in which to hang
clothes in winter. It would pay a man as well as
anything he could build. It would save the wear and
tear on the clothes, besides the health of the ones
who hang them out.

On the other hand, southerner Magnolia Le Guin had a
different feeling about the outdoors and washday:

October 9, 1909
I always welcome wash days because I can get out
doors one half day each week. I ironed today and
I'm nearly exhausted tonight.

Cooking was also a major task. Let's consider the preparation of it, especially at harvest time. Mary Dodge Woodward
has this to say:

August 11, 1885
Harvest has started. Now there will be no rest for
man, woman, or beast until frost which comes,
thank heaven, early here. I was nearly beside myself
getting dinner for thirteen men, besides carpenters
and tinners, with [daughter] Katie sick in bed and
[daughter-in-law] Elsie washing. I baked seventeen
loaves of bread today, making seventy-four since last
Sunday, not to mention twenty-one pies, and pud-
dings, cakes, and doughnuts.

Not to overlook how hard those men were working, she continues: "The men cut one hundred acres today. All four of our harvesters are being used as well as three which were hired to cut by the acre."

Abraham Maslow, among other contemporary psychologists, posits the idea that human beings cannot begin to develop their full human potential until the basic needs have been met: food, shelter, security, and so on. Only then can one focus inward and begin to explore the inner self. Diarists in the centuries before this one usually had pressing physical problems of survival, depending on their class, circumstances, and whereabouts: providing the food, the shelter, and the security for family and self, coping with the sheer logistics of making it safely through the day. These problems usurped their lives, seemed to be what life was about, in fact. The telling of the tasks performed, therefore, represented mind-time as well as physical time and energy spent. Those simple ditto marks add up to weariness and a day well spent, usually in the service of others.

In English gentlewomen's diaries, however, there is little service to others and few feats of physical labour; there is also better spelling and punctuation, a larger, more refined vocabulary, with the occasional literary allusion thrown in, and a more affluent lifestyle, an unknown word then. Were it not for Arthur Munby, there might have been no first-hand knowledge of how a lower-class woman in the nineteenth century spent her time and energy.

Upper-class himself, Arthur Munby, who kept a diary, met Victorian maidservant Hannah Cullwick (1833-1909) when she was twenty. They had a fifty-year secret relationship during which they lived apart and she kept on working. He married her after eighteen years, but she resisted becoming a Victorian lady and they separated after four years, while maintaining the relationship. Hannah deliberately chose below-stairs drudge work because she felt it gave her greater freedom. The reason we know so much about her is that Munby required her to write a diary for him, to describe her drudgery and life. He loved her in her dirt, she says. She called him Massa, their idea of what a master is called by his slave, and she served him like one. At one time she even wore a steel chain and padlock around her neck, to which Munby had the key.

Literate before she knew Munby, Hannah began writing her seventeen diaries for him, as he requested, but as time went on, she did so for other reasons, among them being the influence she gained over her relationship with her husband. Later she quit, also to maintain her control. Obviously, there's more to this than mere telling of tasks, but here is a description of her work on the grate in the presence of her employers:

> The day was *very* hot & so I sweated more nor
> usual, & being look'd at all the time by the ladies
> made me still hotter. I thought I would show them
> how Massa likes me to clean a grate & I ventured
> to rub the bars with my bare hands, & yet I was
> afear'd they may think it a dirty way. But, instead,
> the Miss Knight in bed watch'd me, & spoke quite
> pleasantly, & when she saw I wanted more wet said,

"Come here, Hannah, I'll wet your hand for you out of my bottle." I had taken care to get my arms black & I rubb'd them across my face, & having my striped apron on & frock pinn'd up, you may guess how I look'd as I crawl'd on my knees to & from the bedside & holding my hand up for the water. [Her] been so delicate, as white as a lily & her face too, from been in bed so many years, & I supposed never soil'd her fingers ever, except perhaps with a dirty book or paper, & the white coverlet & all standing out against my dirty black hands, & my *big* red & black arms, & my face red too & sweating till the drops tumbled off, or stood on little drops o' crystal again the greasy black.

I wish'd much that M. could see me for I knew he would o' liked to see me so, & and have loved me the more for it. But still I was satisfied that I was doing it for him & I could give him a nice account of it in my writing.

And she certainly could write! Hannah Cullwick makes the telling of the task downright sensuous.

Good friends Ruth Slate and Eva Slawson, the two young English working-class women striving at the turn of this century to better themselves, had a modicum of education and a great thirst for more. Their writing style in their diaries and letters visibly improves as they make every effort, against great odds, to maintain their intellectual pursuits. They were ardent suffragettes, incipient communists — Slawson in the purest, small-c meaning of the term —

and devoted friends. They went to public meetings and lectures and fed each other books and reviews, hungry for ideas and for more control over their lives. Slawson was the same age as Virginia Woolf, and Slate two years younger, all of them living in England, yet how different their lives were, and their tasks!

Eva Slawson was an illegitimate child and grew up with her grandparents, moving as an adult to live with an aunt. She has more freedom and time than Slate and she has a good job, as a secretary in a solicitor's office. Still, she is bound to her working level by her class and gender. The war begins and she remains faithful to her work. Women's tasks, as we know from other wars, sometimes vary, depending on the availability of men to do them. She cannot refrain from making a comment about women's work:

> Friday, 29 January 1915
> [I]t is suggested women should work upon the
> land. So we may take a share when the world is at
> war, but in time of peace we are not considered
> worthy of political freedom!

On April 20, a fellow worker returns and she writes:

> — it was so nice to see him again. He told me the
> firm had suffered but little through the way, that
> Miss Bone considered they had taken advantage of
> me in every way, first by substituting a bonus for an
> increase in salary, second by stopping the bonus
> owing to the war, and third by giving me Frost's
> work to do as well as my own.

Just after Frost had finished speaking, out came Mr Hazlegrove and informed me that I had used the telephone to the City *twice* yesterday, thus costing the firm *4d*!! Horrors! I felt inclined to point out that at present I am saving them considerably *over 4d* a week! It is such incidents which cast a bitter drop into one's cup — I must try however to rise above a rather sullen feeling which threatens to take possession of me after these experiences.

Slawson would not be surprised to learn that women's tasks still don't get equal recognition or remuneration.

Overworked and constantly exhausted, Ruth Slate returns from her low-paying job to do the housework for her ailing mother and tubercular younger sister, who eventually dies. She receives no help from her brother or father and turns over most of her salary to her mother for room and board. After a rather poor job, she is envied for getting one as a secretarial clerk in the salesroom at a grocer's firm where she stays for twelve years until she is fortunate enough to receive some further education.

In 1906, at the age of twenty-two, Slate becomes engaged to a man who later proves unworthy of her and whose rotten behaviour remains a secret, alluded to but censored. The point here is that, a year after her engagement, three months past the time when she should have had a raise in pay, she reports, "I have been as good as told that I shall not receive one, it being inferred that as an 'engaged' girl, I should not expect it."

Although she constantly tries to improve herself, she confesses her despair to her diary:

Thursday 29th April, 1909
During the evening meeting I could only think
with a certain bitterness of that enormous difference [between her "little knowledge and broad
culture"] and of the unfairness of unequal opportunity. "I have the brains," I thought, "and the willing-
ness to use them, but I have never had the chance."
Even now every little effort of self-improvement
has to be made at the expense of recreation. Why
should it be so?

Self-improvement was a monumental, never-ending task, especially for the working poor.

At the end of the year, Slate goes into lodgings of her own, guilty at being so happy, but more confident and determined eventually to leave her employers, who she feels strongly are exploiting her. In a way, her diary is all tasks, being a record of the constant effort she makes to improve herself.

Virginia Woolf had a productive year in 1908, accord-ing to the spasmodic diaries she was keeping at the time. More than a dozen of her reviews were published in *The Times Literary Supplement*, and *The Cornhill Magazine* print-ed six essays. By February 1909, Woolf finished the first seven chapters of a novel, *The Voyage Out*. The tasks she set herself were paying off. She inherited some money in April and set out for Florence and Milan. In 1912, she married

Leonard Woolf. *The Voyage Out* was published in March 1915. She was having a nice life.

She began a prelude to her diaries in 1915 when she was twenty-eight; it lasted for about six weeks. She took another stab at the diary in the latter part of 1917 and began the sustained effort in 1918. The tasks she reports include her writing, of course, and her book-making with Leonard (Hogarth Press), all just as draining of her energy as more menial repetitive ones, but more creatively satisfying. The wonder of her is that she understood what other women were going through. She wrote *A Room of One's Own* in 1928.

As for the domestic tasks, the Woolfs had servants; it was rare for Virginia to have to do for Leonard and herself. Then, too, she had in Leonard a wife to nurture not only her genius but also her humanity, which few women have ever enjoyed, even to the present day. George Eliot and Colette in her last marriage received similar support. Does a woman have to be a writer and a genius to get it? Katherine Mansfield was both but unlucky, and she knew it. In her diary, she expressed her envy of Virginia:

November 30, 1919
How I envy Virginia; no wonder she can write.
There is always in her writing a calm freedom of expression as though she were at peace — her roof over her, her possessions round her, and her man somewhere within call.

There are two ways to go with this situation of women's never-ending work. One is martyrdom, evidenced today in Super-Woman behaviour and in other centuries by similar feats of overdoing the service to others and by the resentment when overdone is underappreciated. We have clear evidence in earlier diaries of the indignation, bitterness, and even rage this behaviour eventually engenders.

Contemporary diarists are more conscious of their roles and more aware of the options open to them, but just as hard-working at different tasks. The diaries published so far are of special events, specific careers, or ongoing work: first public concert for a pianist; preliminary sketches for a novel-in-progress; a year in the life of a ballerina, an artist, a potter; a trip to Mexico; an abortion; a pregnancy; a terminal illness — one's own or a dear one's. The tasks in all these accounts are specific and also subordinate to the major subject of late twentieth-century diaries: the cultivation of her inner landscape. The diarist's chief task today seems to be to nurture herself since it's clear to her by now that no one else is going to. Besides, nurturing is what women do best. Nurturing has always been women's primary and never-ending task.

Settling for Leftovers

> WOMEN SEEM SO OFTEN TO DENY THEMSELVES
> AND TO NURTURE OTHERS. WE WORRY ABOUT
> BALANCED MEALS FOR OUR CHILDREN AND
> THEN SETTLE FOR THEIR LEFTOVERS FOR
> OUR OWN.
>
> *Michelle Harrison*

Although nurturing of children, husband, and parents is another huge task that women perform, it is mentioned in their diaries less often than one might expect. Perhaps it's such a given that it's automatically discounted. That's what taking care of a family is all about.

Many a diary gets written with a child pottering about, distracting the diarist. Magnolia Le Guin keeps trying to write in her diary in spite of this handicap:

> August 18, 1902
> I have had to write like fighting fire, in extreme
> haste — baby crying as hard as it could and now he
> is in my lap while I am finishing up this. I'm doing
> hard work worrying myself almost helpless every
> day with baby and trying between his naps to do all
> the work I can. I am doing the work of 2 strong
> negroes and no health and strength. Baby wiggles
> so I can't write.

But she feels guilty about neglecting her children:

November 7, 1902
Wish I had time to keep my little fellows clean and
more tidy but I am so overworked these days I am
obliged to let them go more neglected than I am
ever willing to.

On January 5, 1903, Le Guin makes a New Year's
Resolution:

With Myriad of duties staring [at] me from
Christmas to Christmas and with no privacy —
none at all — children around me almost every
stroke of the pen, talking to me, playing like a room
of colts — with nerves unstrung — a very restless
cross baby — in the face of this — more — I am
going to try to keep a diary, this year A.D.

In Le Guin's case, as time runs out and her strength ebbs,
she worries about the kind of care she is giving her children while the babies just keep on coming:

January 23, 1903
A *busy* life! A *busy* life!! A *busy* life!!!....
    Now I am writing, and I have laid two garments
by to sew buttons on and work button holes, but I
glanced over daily paper, semi-weekly journal and
read some in [Wesley Christian] Advocate — now I
am scribbling and the little garments just as bare of
buttons as when I put them by. Ghu [her husband]
is rocking the baby to sleep and keeps at me to do
this and that and the other and I must write a letter
for him. I do most of his writing.

As the years go by, the busy mother writes less and less in her beloved diary, although she keeps trying. It doesn't take a genius to recognize the truth of her prediction on March 3, 1905:

> [S]ince I've been scribbling Ralph and Mary have torn my trunk "topsy turvy," scattered a jar of buttons over the floor, turned half dozen boxes and the contents bottom upwards in my trunk and on the floor and Ralph has whined a good deal. If I did not love to write I'd never do so under such circumstances.

By the fall of the year she's pregnant again with more to do than ever:

> October 7
> I have so much to do between now and January 1906 and I don't see how I can do it all — so many little garments to make and such little time to sew. I've no help and I'm cooking most of the time. I've already hired more sewing done than I ever did one season before (4 dresses for self 3 coats for boys) and must hire about 6 little prs of pants made yet I guess — and then a whole pile of cloth to sew myself. How I am *ever* to get it done I don't know. I don't have no chance some days to sit down to the machine.... How I'll ever get through before the stork's visit I don't know.... If I had enough leisure and less strain I could and would be a better mother in many ways. I have not the time to be a

companion for my children and am to tired to talk with them much of the time.

Perhaps to a later, healthier generation of women who are more able to time and control their reproduction and who have never experienced the horrendous drain on the body of a succession of pregnancies, Le Guin's diary sounds at times like a constant whine, but she also constantly asks God for patience and strength and submissiveness.

Having become a diary-keeping and diary-reading addict, I have learned to spot my own journal for signs in myself I may have missed. There was a time several years ago, about a year after I had undergone major surgery, when I began each entry with a Le Guin kind of statement: "Tired! Tired!! Tired!!!" It turned out I was anaemic and needed iron pills. Now I pay closer attention to what I'm saying and have said. I also pay attention to other diarists. I know from personal experience that what they write often reflects more deeply than they themselves know what they are about.

When Le Guin worries about the future, that is, the immediate future after the birth of the next child, it's a legitimate concern. During her first delivery, she had a "complication" that damaged her. As a result, she is usually prostrate for two or three months post-partum and unable to do much for her family. There is no one to whom she can address this fear, so she turns to her diary:

December 10
Soon another care, another life will be added to my

many many cares and what then? Who will wait on
me? Who will cook meals and make beds for my
family? Who will see after little one till I have
strength to sit up? Who will see kindly after
Mary when Ghu is out?

I do not know who.

At that, Le Guin counts herself blessed. She says more than
once what a "prop" Ghu is to her and comments on how
much he helps her when he can. Her plight is one of
poverty as well as of gender. But the questions she asks are
those concerning nurturing, the basic task that all women
see as their responsibility alone.

American sociologist Elise Boulding calls it "nurturance," the kind of care she says members of a family must
give one another, not leaving it solely to the mother, and
also the kind of care that members of a neighbourhood
must extend to the community at large, not leaving it solely to women. In a public lecture commissioned by the
Vanier Institute of the Family in 1981, Boulding said that
as long as nurturance is defined as women's work and
remains women's role, society will remain rigid and crisis-
prone. "Nurturance has to be a task that is jointly shared
by men and women." She cites American feminist analyst
Dorothy Dinnerstein, who agrees with her that society
will not change until the tasks of nurturing are shared. In
her landmark book, *The Mermaid and the Minotaur*,
Dinnerstein worries about female-dominated child care.
She thinks it guarantees that "women and men will regard
each other, respectively, as silly overgrown children."

Most diarists sense this, when their backs are to the wall. They write their perception of it in resentful tones or complaints, sometimes even with wry humour. Midwife Martha Ballard soldiers on, not without some irritation:

January, 1796
I am very sick but under nesescity [*sic*] of getting breakfast for Mr Ballard and Cyrus. God grant I may have some one to assist me in my business.

Admittedly, there's more than a touch of self-pity in a later report:

May 22, 23, 1798
I have been very unwell. I Eat a little cold puding and Cold milk twice in the coars of the day and perform part of my washing. I Laid myself on the bed in the bedroom was not able to rise from there. My Husband went to bed and not come to see me so I lay there in my Cloaths till 5 hours morn when I made shift to rise. I got the men Breakfast but was not able to Eat a morsel my self till after 3 pm but I finisht my washing. How many times I have been necasatated to rest my self on the bed I am not able to say. God grant me patience to go thro the fatages of this life with fortitude looking forward to a more happy state.

Other diarists use their diaries as Ballard uses hers, as an outlet for their resentment when they feel hard done by. Thus she bitterly records her husband's frowns and neglect of her when she is ill. Ah, but when *he* needs *her*, that's a different story! Her breast heaves with indignation as she reports one incident:

August 28, 1802
My husband returned at Evening from Ballstown much fatagued with his Journey. Had a fitt of shakeing. I heat a Blankett and put it about him at about 3 hour morning. He being relaxed dirtied the Bed. I rose, shirted him and removed the dirty lining. Went to Bed again but was so Cold that I Could not sleep. I rose again before the sun rose. Washt the things which were unclean but felt so unfitt to attend worship that I tarried at home. My famely all attended. O my God when will the Time be when I may have it in my power to go to thy house to worship again?

Martha Ballard had a continuing conflict and estrangement with her son Jonathan. Apparently Jonathan was a hot-tempered man, the cause of his own considerable troubles, and Martha was a strong-minded woman, too proud to ask for help she felt should have been freely given. Martha expresses a universal complaint in a comment about her son: "It is very strange that men cannot behave like rationall beings."

Ballard is not the only one to doubt men's rational qualities. Eva Slawson has a similar remark and a solution: "Some men are blind — pearls scattered before them are wasted. What they need is a surgical operation." Her friend

Ruth Slate puts it more simply than that: "Why are men so dense?" she asks.

Writer Katherine Mansfield turns to paper to vent her feelings about the caretaking she is expected to perform:

Summer, 1913

I suppose I'm a bad manager, and the house seems to take up so much time if it isn't looked after with some sort of method. I mean ... when I have to clear up twice over or wash up extra unnecessary things I get frightfully impatient and want to be working. So often this week, I've heard you [her husband, John Middleton Murry, and a guest] talking while I washed dishes. Well, someone's got to wash dishes and get food. Otherwise — "There's nothing in the house but eggs to eat." Yes, I hate hate *hate* doing these things that you accept just as all men accept of their women. I can only play the servant with a very bad grace indeed. It's all very well for females who have nothing else to do....

This isn't fair of her at all, regarding other women, but she wasn't feeling fair, she was feeling put-upon.

Yet women serve and honour their mates, as women are expected to do, and they try not to let any dissatisfaction or trouble leak outside the family walls. What will people think? Loyalty to her husband and pride in herself makes a woman unwilling to admit that her man has been less than honourable in his dealings with her, which is why it's still so repugnant to a victim of wife-battering to lay charges against her husband. It is a "secret to be burried," as Emily Gillespie says. Most women still feel it's their fault, that they have been remiss somehow, not nurturant enough. Conflicting views about nurturance surface in contemporary women's diaries.

American writer Kate Green kept an abortion journal in 1977, a private journal, she says, that became "a public piece of writing." At the clinic where she goes to be tested, to confirm her suspicion that she is pregnant, and to make arrangements if she is, she writes:

> It's not that I don't want a baby, just not now. I have
> fantasies — love and a blue tablecloth. Willie and
> me in a small apartment over by the lake. But we're
> not even living together. Don't even know if we
> want to. Haven't got that far yet.

Already she has an inkling of what responsibility means. The next day when she tells her boyfriend and announces that she has already made the appointment at the clinic, she concludes: "We play at love. Being pregnant makes that clear." For six days she nurtures the foetus in her womb:

> This is as close as you come to earth. Near the door
> but forever held in me. They say there is something
> of heaven in that dark curling heart. This blue you
> will never see, your father you will never feel. His
> hands, his music. Single song, hum of fly, afternoon
> alive, baby in my womb.

Abigail Lewis (b. 1923, not her real name) was told by her

doctors that she would never have children. In 1948, two years after she married, well launched into a career in ceramic sculpture, she discovers to her dismay that she is pregnant. She keeps a journal of her pregnancy and learns her first hard lessons in nurturance. Contrary to the stereotype, she finds it doesn't come naturally. Abigail questions everything, especially men's attitudes. When asked whether she plans to continue graduate school or to take her "duties as a wife more seriously," she bursts out:

> September 7, Tuesday
> Damn men and their conception of duty too! Is it being an irresponsible wife to want to get an education?... How much does a wife owe to herself and how much to her husband? I thought I knew, but now I find it takes a lot of thought, time, and effort to make even such a makeshift home as ours. I have often thought of getting a job.... I would be afraid of it splitting my interests.

Her resentment grows with her discomfort. Unable to sleep one night, she goes downstairs to read until her husband complains that he can't sleep! Her response in her diary echoes the spoken and unspoken indignation of women over the centuries:

> February 10, Thursday
> There should be a special course for prospective fathers, especially when they are the ones who profess to want the child.... *All* women want children, of course. What else is there for them in life? And if

the poor creatures happen to be ill, or despairing, or unable to sleep, the men complain because *their* sleep is spoiled.

Now that she's rolling she gets up a good head of steam:

> [H]e comes into the kitchen and backs out as if he had just stepped on a toad, exclaiming that the floor is just filthy. Of course it is. I had rather hoped he would notice it and volunteer to wash it of his own accord, because there happen to be a couple of feet in my ribs that keep me from bending over. He replies that he has heard that scrubbing floors is good for pregnant women.

Once the baby is born Lewis needs time to get used to the whole idea of motherhood:

> FOUR WEEKS OLD: The role of mother is too strange to me. I don't think I could ever be primarily a mother without sacrificing a large part of myself, which I am certainly not prepared to do and don't think is really necessary or desirable. But that first dinner [out, with her husband] showed me I could compromise a little on my motherhood and that my world was not entirely lost.

Not to lose oneself, that is part of nurturance now, to cherish and nurture one's own development. Abigail Lewis projects into the future as she realizes that her infant will one day be an adult and hopes she will not be resentful that "when aging forty-five she will be in the most enchanted and difficult period of life, in the full glory and terror of life. May she meet it well...."

What Lewis doesn't realize, because she is nowhere near an "aging forty-five" herself, is that by that time she will probably have other responsibilities of nurturing — her parents.

Magnolia Le Guin gave that kind of nurturing to both her parents, in whose home she and her family lived after the death of her first child. Her concern about her mother and father interleave the pages with her child-care problems. She reports on their illnesses and their relationship with the children and on her feelings of guilt that she is not doing enough for them or that she is too impatient with them. Dr. and Mrs. Wynn opposed their daughter's preference for Ghu Le Guin and she was torn, or so she says in a few scant early entries, between displeasing her parents and breaking Ghu's heart. Allowed to marry in November 1892, the couple lived near Ghu's family in Peeksville, Georgia. In 1894, after her first baby dies at three days of age, she and her husband move in with her parents and stay.

Over the years, Dr. Wynn comes to trust Ghu to the point of naming him co-executor of his will and leaving the Le Guins the home, the mill, and part of the farm. But relations must have been strained for a few years. Magnolia doesn't mention her parents in her diary until October 1902, when her father is sick and she hopes he'll be "spared for a long time yet to his children and grand children.

"Mama hasn't been well in some time," Le Guin adds.

"She looks bad." After that her parents are included in her concerns. She must have made a conscious decision to change her behaviour towards them and to nurture them as well. We get some indication of this after the deaths of both the old people in 1911 when, among only ten entries and in the longest one for the entire year, Le Guin concludes:

> August 29
> I suffer remorse and will as long as I live for six
> years of a back-slidden [*sic*] life of my own. Six dark
> years — after I became a mother — six dark years
> in sin in my mother and father's life when I should
> have been a great blessing to them, and I suffer
> remorse because I was so led by Evil Agent as not
> to be a loving obedient, patient, sympathetic, dutiful
> daughter to them in all ways I should have been.

Guilt feelings are one of the surest signs of an ingrained acknowledgement of responsibility for nurturing services. In May 1980, contemporary American diarist Darlene Myers, feeling alone and guilty for not being a better daughter, writes in her diary about the last month of her mother's life:

> Wednesday
> The nurse sent me to get Pampers for her because
> her control was getting progressively worse. I went
> to the store with the idea of buying them because
> it would be easier on the nurses, but when I came
> to the conclusion that Mother deserves some

dignity and does have some sense of what and who she is now, more than ever before, I went home not buying them.

Nurturance takes many forms.

Nearing forty, American writer Le Anne Schreiber keeps a journal during a crucial time in hers and her mother's life: her first year on her own as a freelance writer and her mother's last year of life. Because she has left her regular job, Schreiber is free to spend more time than she might have with her parents during her mother's terminal cancer and to track her own feelings. She provides us with some further insights into nurturance:

Wednesday, September 4, 1985
I have never been able to stand the sight of Mom
in pain. I respond to it bodily.

Schreiber's parents lived in Minnesota, Le Anne in New York. She has to make arrangements to spend time away, so she needs a "clear sense of Mom's odds." Her father is already there; her brother, a doctor, can't rearrange his commitments. She writes: "They could afford to remain innocent; I couldn't. I had to plan for Mom's death, and I had to do it in stealth." Such stealth is a form of nurturance.

Schreiber realizes, slowly, that she has to nurture her father as well, as she senses his concern about his own health. What she recognizes first is "the camouflage suit of an honorary woman." All our stereotypes die hard. Schreiber sees her father become "a caregiver, adept at meeting needs before they are spoken. He cooks, he washes dishes, he cleans house, he does laundry, and he does it well, without complaint or illusions of moral grandeur."

Nurturance, she discovers, is not exclusive to the female. Nor is guilt. Guilt seems to be a given during some crises but it can be eased somewhat, as when Schreiber is leaving after a visit and her mother rallies to try to reassure her that it's all right to go:

> Monday, May 5
> Ever since I've been old enough to compare her to other mothers, I have marveled at my good fortune in being born to a woman without a guilt-inducing bone in her body. This doesn't spare me guilt, but it spares me the redoubled pangs of being angry at the object of my guilt.

These are all records of domestic experience, life in the here and now, day by day by day. "Life is so daily," says Anna, a character in my play *Mark*. "Why can't I get used to it?" The question is whether women ever do get used to it. What they often do instead is escape — into the pages of a diary, or farther out into the world.

CHAPTER FOUR

Self-Discovery

I KNOW THAT THE JOURNEY IS NEVER
WHAT WE PLAN FOR; IT'S WHAT HAPPENS
BETWEEN THE LINES.

Mary Morris

Women are perceived as homebodies. Their lives over centuries have taken place in rooms, within doors. They seem to have been content or at least able to function, to keep on doing what they have to do. Who knows what fantasies they have imagined, not only of the Prince but of strange adventures and far-away places? Few of them have ever managed to realize those dreams; even those who succeeded found it hard. "It is not easy to move through the world alone," notes contemporary American writer Mary Morris in *Nothing to Declare*, a travel memoir based on her diary, "and it is never easy for a woman. You must keep your wits about you." (As if a woman didn't always have to keep her wits about her!)

Geographical travel is a form of escape, of course, although the traveller soon learns that she cannot leave herself behind. Her response to the external world may come as a surprise as she discovers things about herself. So too, but more expectedly, with an inner journey, in which a woman tries to discover her own inner landscape: the discoveries she makes are intensely personal — and world-shaking. In any case, warns Morris, "Brace yourself for tremendous emptiness and great surprise."

Breaking Down the Inner Structure

Albert Camus

The Intrepid Travellers are diarists who seem to be most exempt from tasks and the telling of them. They form a subculture of their own. None of them seem to need husbands, although some acquire or lose them. Most of them discover that it is more convenient not to have babies while travelling. The adventurous English lepidopterist Margaret Fountaine, for example, had a long-term relationship with an Eastern dragoman fifteen years her junior (until she discovered that he was already married), but she was never encumbered with babies. A few of the married travellers are initially reluctant to leave home, to be spirited away to exotic places by husbands in some business or other: missionary work, diplomacy, foreign affairs, farming. Although such women cannot be considered such doughty voyagers when someone forced them to go, they occasionally enjoyed the scenery in spite of the fact that most of them were dragged along for the wagon ride by their husbands.

As the close of the nineteenth century saw women on both sides of the Atlantic begin to fight for the franchise, so it also saw a phalanx of fearless females sally forth to explore the world. Most of them seem to have had some independent income, usually an inheritance from the family or a conveniently deceased husband. The point is, they were fancy-free and delighted with everything. Actually, women have been travelling and writing about it for sixteen centuries; adventures were not limited to those English ladies armed, as one writer put it, with a passport and a parasol. Discounting the emigrants, missionaries, pioneering wives, and even some inadvertent explorers, the records of the tourists abound. Most of these women kept accounts, or diaries, or journals, often in the form of letters sent home at every opportunity to eliminate the need of carrying all that paper around with them, but they were intended more as personal journals than as communication.

Ditzy English spinster Isabella Bird (1831–1904) is the perfect stereotype of the intrepid Victorian traveller and one of the most prolific. She spent the first forty years of her life looking after her parents and began to travel initially for reasons of health. Obviously, travel agreed with her, according to her enthusiastic published reports about her adventures in Hawaii, the American Rockies, Japan, Persia, Kurdistan, Tibet, and China, among others. She was the first woman to be invited to address a meeting of the exclusive (read: male) Royal Geographical Society in 1892, and the first of fifteen pioneering women to be elected to fellowship in the society.

In her delightful diary, *A Lady's Life in the Rocky Mountains*, she keeps claiming she doesn't feel the cold as she traipses alone around the Colorado Rockies in 1873, wearing her flannel Hawaiian riding habit:

> For the benefit of other lady travelers, I wish to explain that my "Hawaian riding dress" is the "American Lady's Mountain Dress," a half-fitting jacket, a skirt reaching to the ankles, and full Turkish trousers gathered into frills falling over the boots — a thoroughly serviceable and feminine costume for mountaineering and other rough traveling, as in the Alps or any other part of the world. [Author's note to the second edition, November 27, 1879.]

She covered some 800 miles, alone most of the time and without enough sense to come in out of a blizzard. Her wet hair freezes and she gets frostbite in the hand she keeps bare so as to pick open one frozen eyelid to see her way through the storm. Spending up to ten hours in the saddle some days, with a handful of raisins for food, she catches chills because of clothing that is inadequate or increasingly threadbare or damp because she hasn't given it time to dry after washing. With delicious sang-froid she will describe a trail that sends her horse down, and her with it, rolling over a "shelf of three feet of descent." She suffers more falls as she skirts a ravine — "the dry bed of some awful torrent; there were huge shelves of rock, great overhanging walls of rock, great prostrate trees, cedar spikes and cacti to wound the feet, and then a precipice fully 500 feet deep!"

The quintessential tourist, she writes exquisite descriptions of sunrises, sunsets, and mountains with boundless enthusiasm and a short memory: everything is the biggest, best, most beautiful she has ever seen. While stopping without plan at whatever accommodation she can find, where the sheets might freeze to her body and her ink most certainly does freeze, she records her adventures.

Once a cactus spine penetrates her foot, "some vicious thing" cuts her neck, and yet Isabella Bird feels sorry for a female companion who is with her only briefly: "Poor Mrs. C. was much bruised, and I pitied her, for she got no fun out of it as I did." This particular excursion was one of the rare times the migratory Bird had travelling companions. Mrs. C.'s husband was supposed to be finding a trail to Colorado's national park, Estes Park, but he kept going in the wrong direction. Bird finally took over and found the way back to where they started, forgiving the man in her account of the failed venture: "Though he failed so grotesquely, he did his incompetent best."

When she finally found the park, alone, she was snowed in for the winter in a mountain cabin, with two young men. Another even younger, more selfish and incompetent man arrives who makes their ordeal more arduous. The group was challenged to survive. Bird describes their efforts with the dwindling food and fuel supply with matter-of-fact good humour, although she gets angry at the selfish newcomer who steals food they can't spare. She also describes

several meetings with Rocky Mountain Jim, a gentleman-
ly desperado who is hiding out for whatever misdeeds he
had committed and with whom she has delightful conver-
sations. Her parting from him is harder than her departure
from her Rocky Mountain life. He leads her out, reciting
poetry, including some he had written himself, and she
urges him to change his ways before it is too late.

> I knew that no one else could or would speak to
> him as I could, and for the last time I urged upon
> him the necessity of a reformation in his life.… "Too
> late! too late!" he always answered, "for such a change."
> … I have seen [he has] with a single exception, a
> gentleness, propriety, and considerateness of manner
> surprising in any man, but especially so in a man
> associating only with the rough men of the West.

Her last glimpse of him is as he leads her horse back to Estes
Park, "with his golden hair yellow in the sunshine." It is not
hard to read between the lines and realize that the lady has
half fallen in love with the wild man.

Anna Brownell Jameson (1794–1860) left England in
1836 to join her husband, Robert Jameson, then the attor-
ney general of Upper Canada (Ontario). Apparently she
travelled to the New World not out of devotion but to
arrange a permanent, formal separation. Her diary recording her winter in Toronto and her summer trip through
Ontario was published on her return to England in 1838.
Like Isabella Bird's, her ink froze as she wrote, and she
feared for her faculties as well as her fingers:

January 16, 1837
This will never do! — I *must* rouse myself to occupation; and if I cannot find it without, I must create it from within. There are yet four months of winter and leisure to be disposed of.

But she did dispose of them and stayed long enough to explore Ontario in the summer by a combination of inconvenient and unreliable modes of travel: a private carriage trip west to London, though on "a very rough road for a carriage, [is] a delightful ride." She takes a carriage to Hamilton, then a steamboat across Lake Ontario to Niagara (four hours in "a strange darkness," just ahead of a storm), then on an impulse, a "turbulent" ferry to Buffalo, and on returning, a public stage-coach back to Niagara and Hamilton ("tumbling along the detestable road"). Jameson deplores the lack of a train: "What would not a railroad do for them here?" At Hamilton once again she hires a light wagon and a man to drive her to Brandtford [*sic*], about twenty-five miles, for five dollars. "The country all the way was rich, and beautiful," Jameson writes, "— the roads abominable as could be imagined to exist. So I then thought, but have learned since that there are degrees of badness in this respect, to which the human imagination has not yet descended."

From "Brandtford" (its namesake was still acknowledged), she proceeds to Paris and Woodstock, admiring the scenery and cursing the "execrably bad" roads. She dines on milk and eggs at farmhouses in the absence of inns, arriving finally at Blandford, having taken nine hours to travel twenty-five miles, where she is welcomed by a farm family who have been expecting her. Next she hires a baker's cart to take her to London, a further thirty miles (for seven dollars), thence to St. Thomas, "one of the prettiest places I had yet seen," and Port Talbot, where Colonel Talbot is expecting her. After six days' rest, Jameson's next journey was from Port Talbot to Chatham, then across Lake St. Clair, on a "little steam-boat" to Detroit, arriving at sunset. A tourists' ailment confines her in her hotel room for three days, causing her to miss the steamer to Mackinac Island, for which she must wait another six days. Finally she arrives at the island, with, for a change, no letters of introduction, and as the steamer glides away, Jameson is overwhelmed by loneliness: "a momentary wonder and alarm to find myself so far from any human being who took the least interest about my fate." This is a revelation coming from one of the intrepids who busies herself with reporting the external world.

Of course, she found people and had a delightful visit to Sault Ste. Marie. She was sorry to leave as she takes another lake voyage to Manitoulin Island, a three-day camping trip. She had hoped for a birch-bark canoe, but by this time her party had grown and they were encumbered with baggage and provisions, so she was supplied with a "bateau." On reaching the island, Jameson was greeted with the news that the King (William IV) was dead and Queen Victoria reigned in his place.

"It is of the woman I think, more than of the queen," writes Jameson.

Travelling down Lake Huron, Jameson finally got her wish: a ride in a birch-bark canoe down the lake. "There were two canoes," she reports, "each five-and-twenty feet in length, and four feet in width, tapering to the two extremities, and light, elegant and bouyant as the sea-mew when it skims the summer waves." She was taken by water all the way to the bay of Penetanguishene, where she was pleased to be lodged in an inn and to be able to "sleep once more on a christian bed.

"But nine nights passed in the open air, or on rocks and on boards, had spoiled me for the comforts of civilisation, and to sleep on a *bed* was impossible; I was smothered, I was suffocated, and altogether wretched and fevered; — I sighed for my rock on Lake Huron."

She continued by water to Lake Simcoe, fishing in Lake Couchiching on the way, and admiring the rapids of the river Severn, too exhausted with all the superlatives of her trip to be eloquent. At Lake Simcoe she took another steamer, proceeding down to Holland Landing, where she disembarked, "and the rest of the way lay through the Home District, and through some of the finest land and most prosperous estates in Upper Canada" — with an "excellent road," called Yonge Street, leading to the capital.

"At three o'clock in the morning, just as the moon was setting in Lake Ontario, I arrived at the door of my own house in Toronto, having been absent on this wild expedition just two months."

But the conveyances and the scenery are the least of Anna Jameson's travelogue. She discusses politics and economics as well as scenery, history as well as weather, and the state of women in the New World, including native women. She is far more concerned with the quality of life than of the roads, and of the relationship between men and women in a harsh new setting. Wherever she travels, she brings her own lively curiosity and critical faculties to bear on what she meets.

She travelled alone, with the odd letter of introduction to pave her way, and of course, with enough money and status to ensure her safe accommodation. Even so, she comments one evening on her state: "It is midnight and I am alone; and if I do not feel fear, I feel at least the want of a supporting arm, the want of a sustaining heart."

After her brief visit to Canada, she returned to England and published *Winter Studies and Summer Rambles in Canada* (1838) and kept herself busy with art history for the rest of her life, alone. She died in London, England, at the age of sixty-six.

Margaret Fountaine toured the world with delight and impunity. She was only a poor clergyman's daughter, but her mother's brother made a fortune as possibly the first manufacturer of artificial fertilizers in the world. His provision for his widowed sister's children gave Fountaine the independence to collect her butterflies all over the world.

The passionate spinster is quite frank about her sensuous pleasures:

Giayoni, 1901
We [her guide and she] halted in an olive garden at
a place called Kafr Kenna (the supposed Cana of

Galilee) where a church is now built over the place, where the miracle is said to have happened. Two large, stone water-pots are shown in this church, which were excavated from the ground beneath — I thought it would have been more conclusive had they found six. I did feel a thrill when I stood on this spot which tradition has selected as the scene of our Lord's first miracle. But earthly love was greater, and the kiss my lover gave me in the olive garden later in the afternoon was so full of passionate tenderness that it should not be passed over in silence.

Fountaine sails to Crete in 1902 without her dragoman and reports being flattered by the propositions of an Egyptian ship's officer, "[who] when I refused to accompany him to the heart of Asia Minor, promptly told me I looked forty, thereby exactly hitting the right nail on the head, though of course I instantly denied it." In Crete she starts off on horseback with a muleteer and a guide.

All that day we rode on without seeing a sign of the *Lycaena Psylorita*, the rare little butterfly I had come to Crete to capture. At mid-day we halted at a monastery, where the monks provided me with a lunch of poached eggs and bread.... By and by we pushed on. I had never ridden over such infamously rough mountain tracks before. My little horse fell with me twice and had I been riding in the usual fashion for ladies, which I have long since found to be quite impracticable in these countries, nothing could have saved me from being pitched off head foremost on to the rocks.

Though these women had in common a great wanderlust, they differed from one another in their attitudes and reactions as well as in what they chose to see. They all, however, do tend to notice what other women are doing or suffering, and with some sympathy. They give themselves away in this, as being more sensitive than a tourist and more introspective than a dilettante. Though greedy for experience, they see the world without rose-coloured glasses, perhaps with the exception of Isabella Bird.

Mary Schäffer Warren (1861–1939) was born Mary Sharples in Philadelphia. A Quaker with an independent attitude and a gentlewoman's education (i.e., with some training in drawing and watercolours), she married an older man, Dr. Charles Schäffer, a medical doctor who was more interested in botany. After his death in 1903 and the death of her parents in the same year, Mary Schäffer set about providing her own secure income through investments and then devoted herself to finishing her late husband's life project, a book about wildflowers. To do that she had to learn to use a camera and to ride a horse. The couple's quest had taken them to the Canadian Rockies before, but they had never ventured far from civilization. Schäffer hired a guide, William "Billy" Warren, nineteen years her junior, to toughen her up, teach her to ride, and help her find the wildflowers for the book. From a hatred and fear of horses, bears, and all things wild (except those flowers), this tenderfoot developed a passion for the wilderness. She writes in a later journal: "Civilization! How little it means when one has tasted the free life of the trail!"

In 1907 *Alpine Flora of the Canadian Rocky Mountains* was published by G.P. Putnam's and sold for $3. Schäffer had enlisted the help of a trained botanist, Stewardson Brown, and she supplied the illustrations from her own watercolour drawings and photographs. By that time she was hooked.

In 1907 and 1908, with her guide and a camp cook, Schäffer and a woman friend explored some old trails, just for the fun of it, and she kept a journal of both expeditions. In it she boasts that she has learned how to wash a blanket in a teacup of water, but it's clearly a lark. She is on holiday. She pays the men to do for her while she and her friend enjoy the scenery.

Later, in a book based on her journals, she published an account of these two trail rides. *Old Indian Trails of the Canadian Rockies*, with photographs, was published by G.P. Putnam's in 1911 (price, $2) but is long since out of print. During the second trip, following a rough map sketched by a native friend, Schäffer and her party "discovered" Maligne Lake.

In 1911, in recognition of Schäffer's discovery, the Canadian government asked her to survey the lake, ignoring her protests that she didn't know how. So she did and kept another journal, not published until after her death. *A Hunter of Peace: Old Indian Trails of the Canadian Rockies*, edited by E.J. Hart, was published by The Whyte

Foundation, Banff, Alberta, in 1980, and includes excerpts from the earlier diaries.

For the survey trip, Schäffer took her sister-in-law and nephew with a different guide, the same cook, and the makings of the boat she would need to survey the lake. By that time the train went as far as Jasper, so she and her family met her guide there. On the first night out on the trail, before they head up into the mountains, she sees the wagon trains going by, on their way to open up the Canadian West.

Schäffer notices one particular woman sitting with her man "on top of an extra heavy load ... she with a face that told of hardship, poverty, loyalty, all the wordless misery which goes to make up the life of the pioneer woman." The diarist draws her own conclusion from what she sees:

> And the world goes on singing the praises of the
> pioneer, the "man who opens the door." Could he
> open it if the woman did not hand him the key?
> Not from what I have seen.

Mary Schäffer married her guide, Billy Warren, and lived in Banff, Alberta, until her death in 1939.

We might classify some of the travel diarists' tours as more than adventure, rather verging on hardship or peril, except that they seem to thrive on it. Isabella Bird, for example, was having fun. Anna Jameson was acting as a reporter, bringing back news from the New World, but she loved her canoe trips. Mary Schäffer Warren calls herself a carefree tourist, not an explorer. She never named a mountain after herself, but she did call one after her young nephew Paul, and it's still on the map. Hardship is in the perception of the one who endures it, apparently. One woman's ordeal is another woman's pleasure.

Just as men diarists kept their journals for different reasons and with different effect, so the travellers differed too. Even the tourists take time to comment on social conditions and to wonder about women like themselves. Contemporary English writer Jane Robinson, who has published a book cataloguing the women travellers (*Wayward Women*), offers this comment as an overgeneralization, but worth keeping in mind when reading women's travelogues: "Men's travel accounts are traditionally concerned with What and Where, and women's with How and Why."

American travel writer Mary Morris has experienced the fantasy realized of adventurous travel but she is also aware of what happens when a woman embarks on such a journey. The trip outward doesn't necessarily end up outside oneself. She has realized, as many travellers do who sought only escape, that they have encountered countries not recorded on any existing maps. Using this metaphor, Morris welcomes such a discovery: "Sometimes it is difficult, but I try to read other maps. Maps of my own inner landscape, of dreams and of the outcome of the events of my life, of the warnings and signs of others.... [I]f I pay attention, I am right, and these maps of my own instincts guide me as surely as any Rand McNally would."

Sooner or later, perhaps every diarist will discover this, that all roads lead to inner space.

The Middle of a Landscape

EVERYBODY LIVES IN THE MIDDLE OF A LAND-
SCAPE. WRITING CAN PROVIDE A MAP.

Phyllis Theroux

Inner journeys may not look nearly as active or exciting as geographical ones, but they can offer discoveries to the diarist. Arguably the twentieth century's most famous diarist, Anaïs Nin has been credited with changing the focus of diaries from outer life to inner life, but she was not the first to do so. Before the turn of the century, the young Russian artist Marie Bashkirtseff (1860–1884) revealed herself outrageously in her naïvely immodest diary. She shocked New England spinster Alice James, who reported to her diary that she would have none of her, calling her "the perverse of the perverse." Paula Modersohn-Becker, on the other hand, was stimulated:

> November 15, 1898
> The journal of Marie Bashkirtsev [*sic*]. Her
> thoughts enter my bloodstream and make me very
> sad. I say as she does: if only I could accomplish
> something!

Ten days later the German artist is exhausted from a heavy session of work: "I certainly have a gigantic bear of a hangover from painting.... Marie Bashkirtsev, she's the one I accuse."

Ahead of her time, Bashkirtseff was among the first

diarists to create herself in her own image. Perhaps, considering what the world does to uppity women, she was fortunate to die young, of tuberculosis, at the age of twenty-four.

Canadian writer Elizabeth Smart (1913–1986) used her diaries as a springboard for *By Grand Central Station I Sat Down and Wept* (1945), which has been called one of the finest prose poems of this century, honing introspection to an art. In her journal, Smart apologized: "Each bit could be so much better, if I sat and thought and turned over before I wrote." But she defended herself and it: "It is a diary. It is a preparation." Canadian-born, she lived alone in England and on her own raised four children (by poet George Barker, who had a wife). Late in life she came home to be honoured for her writing, though in her later work she never matched the power of the story of her illicit love affair. She died in England at the age of seventy-three.

These diarists were among the first to practise the kind of introspection so popular today in women's diaries. A few others before them fell into it, often through some distancing, not of their own choosing. These accidental mavericks, outside the system for whatever reason, began questioning the system; they included the invalids, the artists, and occasionally the lady travellers.

An invalid, French novelist and playwright Marie Lénéru always refused to compromise with life:

June 7, 1903
The magnificent thing is to keep my uncompromising attitude with regard to the superfluous,

when I am so lacking in what is necessary. I have
not yet reached the point where I can let myself
slip into a commonplace happiness, but shall I be
able to dispense with it always?

Lonely and angry, Lénéru had been forced to learn acceptance in a hard school: "I accept the past and I love it for
having made me what I am: exceptional." It also made her
discriminating about misfortune:

> August 15, 1902
> I love only those who have regrets, but real regrets.
> Trifling misfortunes, little disappointments —
> heart-troubles, for example, make me cruel. I love
> those who have been really deceived, robbed —
> those who have a very ugly and heartfelt grimace
> to make at existence.

She would not allow her suffering to define her:

> September 9, 1899
> Suffering is a degradation. We make an absurd merit
> of our "having suffered," since necessity assumes
> exclusive responsibility for accomplishing this.

A victim of mere chance, Lénéru resisted alternatives, preferring always to remain an outsider:

> November 9, 1902
> I refuse consolations, *I want to have lost nothing.*"

It's easier for the mavericks to find their way to an inner
landscape. The others, the "safe" ones, the ones who seem

never to be alone, can't afford to withdraw their investment in their life's work. Where would they go? What would they do? Who would they be? Not much choice there, come right down to it. So they stay where they are, and keep on working, like Magnolia Le Guin and all the other quiet, unknown women, the "home-concealed" women attempting to define themselves with a scrap of paper and a scratchy pen. They enter their daily code, hoping to make sense of it all — or not.

Two diarists in this century consciously set out to make sense of it all, that is, to make themselves the entire content of a journal, in a searching self-scrutiny. An ocean and forty years apart, they had a similar purpose: to find out exactly who they were, apart from any scripts written for them.

Marion Milner was born in London, England, in 1900. She had been training for work with young children when, at the age of twenty-six, she decided to keep a diary "of what I wanted and what made me happy," thinking it wouldn't take very long, perhaps a few months. This exploration of self took her seven years, after which she returned to her studies and took a degree in psychology and physiology at London University and became a practising psychoanalyst. *A Life of One's Own*, based on the journal of her experiences, was published in 1934 under a pseudonym, Joanna Field, and a companion volume, *An Experiment in Leisure*, in 1937. Both books were reprinted in 1986, and then in 1987, under the name of Marion (Blackett) Milner, *Eternity's Sunrise: A Way of Keeping a Diary* was published as a sequel to *A Life of One's Own*.

Milner discovers self-confidence in her journey. She recognizes her problem first as one of "relaxing when among other people," and she realizes that she needs to have "some basis of security" before she can; otherwise, her guard will be up. She has already discovered that she can lose herself in music, nature, and so on. However, she still fears the thought of losing her self, that is, her self-consciousness, with another person. Finally she realizes that security is within herself, the self that she is getting to know so well.

She writes, "The idea occurred to me that until you have, once at least, faced everything you know — the whole universe — with utter giving in, and let all that is 'not you' flow over and engulf you, there can be no lasting sense of security." She must lose herself in order to gain security, in order to gain her self.

"I began to guess," Milner writes, "that my self's need was for an equilibrium, for sun, but not too much, for rain, but not always…. So I began to have an idea of my life, *not as the slow shaping of achievement to fit my preconceived purposes, but as the gradual discovery and growth of a purpose which I did not know.*"

She realizes early on that the search is not going to be easy. She writes: "It will mean walking in a fog for a bit, but it's the only way which is not a presumption, forcing the self into a theory."

This kind of exploration was entirely conscious and single-minded. Milner's stated intention from the outset was self-analysis, to find out what she knew about herself and how she knew what she knew, and above all, what was really important. What she discovers is that it is too easy "to blind one's eyes to what one really likes, to drift into accepting one's wants ready-made from other people, and to evade the continual day-to-day sifting of values...."

The worst pitfall, she warns, is "to find [her]self more of a fool than [she] thought." What she describes is a long, difficult journey, among the first and still one of the most exciting and rewarding for anyone who dares to read her journal. No reading between the lines here. She hands us the clues.

In the fall of 1962, at the age of thirty-seven, American teacher Alice Koller (b. 1925) took a puppy with her to Nantucket, where she retreated to find herself through self-analysis in her journal. She concludes with satisfaction at the end of her three-month exploration: "I realize now that no one will ever again be able to tell me something about myself that I don't already know."

Both Milner and Koller are frightened at the outset by their lack of self-knowledge. Milner carefully records daily events, recalls memories of when she was happy and makes lists of things she likes and wants to do, as she tries to discover what it is she really needs.

Similarly, Alice Koller, after "thirty-seven years of not knowing what the hell I'm doing," writes: "I must find some way to know what I think.... I don't know how I respond to things. I don't know how to find out what's going on inside me.... I don't know what to look for inside me."

Once she found what she was looking for, and the way inside, she left this "map" for others to follow her route. Her diary, *An Unknown Woman*, edited after her exploration, was not published until 1982. Koller subtitled it *A Journey to Self-Discovery*.

Until recently, women have had no such maps or manuals to guide them from generation to generation because their records were all but obliterated. Each generation had to make its own map and learn to read it. The subject of women's journals didn't change but the direction did. The journey now goes inward. We can read of the tasks, the stories, and the search. By careful reading, we can interpret earlier messages and find the thread of continuity.

Professional training isn't necessary for a diarist to set out on this trail of self-discovery. At present, the only contemporary diaries that are available to us are the public ones, that is, the published ones; these are by writers, therapists, women with a specific, urgent story to tell, and sell. Other, more private women are writing and they, too, are intent on discovery. Thus they come out of the darkness, seeking illumination as they open the I/eye. All it takes is time.

Surprising Strides

IT IS A MISTAKE TO REGARD AGE AS A DOWN-
HILL GRADE TOWARD DISSOLUTION. THE
REVERSE IS TRUE. AS ONE GROWS OLDER ONE
CLIMBS WITH SURPRISING STRIDES.

George Sand

A diarist may be surprised to find that her age presents no obstacle to discovery and recovery of self. Age, in fact, seems to present an opportunity to some aging diarists, not the aging, but simply — age.

Old women have had bad press. *Crone* once meant "wise old woman"; men's language has reduced it to "ugly old hag." Women see themselves with men's eyes, so a mirror gives them an image they find repulsive. Philadelphia Quaker and long-time diarist Deborah Norris Logan chanced to look into a mirror on September 15, 1838. She writes:

> Passing by a glass in one of the chambers just now, I was perfectly shocked to see myself — so old and so ugly. But what else can be expected at seventy-seven! Never mind. Take courage. Nobody expects to find any beauty or even "agreeableness" at that age. But they may look perhaps for a little sense — and so farewell to this foolery.

This is, after all, someone else's way of seeing her, of judging her. The diary may yield a truer image, that of the person she has been searching for all her life. Diary as mirror.

How do women cope with being old in their diaries? They must look at their faces and read their own lines. Here is a woman at the end of her life, and if it's not the end, it feels like it. Totally invisible to men, neglected and/or rejected by society, which is run by men, loved perhaps but not listened to by her family, the old woman, like many younger ones, continues to be passive, to be done to, even put upon. She is an object in, not the subject of, her own life.

> January 24, 1888
> I like a farm better than a home in town; however, for the rest of my days I do not expect to be considered nor consulted as to where I should rather live.

Thus, Mary Dodge Woodward bowed to the inevitable, two years before her death, as it turned out. She concludes this entry by stating her resolve: "I'll keep up with the procession as long as I'm able."

After she was widowed at fifty-six, Woodward left Wisconsin, where she had moved from Vermont with her husband to raise their five children, and settled farther west with three of her children in Fargo, Dakota Territory. On June 27, 1886, she wrote:

> My sixtieth birthday. I can scarcely believe that I am nearing the time allotted to mortals. But I am very glad to think that no one would suffer were I to shuffle off this mortal coil.

In other centuries, other places, old women were drowned or burned as witches, or force-fed to their husband's funeral pyre, or expected to go gently into the Arctic night, or, in later centuries, put away in asylums, kept docile with Valium, or taken care of with inadequate pensions. Because women live longer, older ones seldom find themselves in the keeping of men. Mostly they do for themselves, as best they can. The remarkable thing is the equanimity with which many of them face it, more centred, more focused, and — after they get used to it — savouring the solitude.

It's a carefully cultivated attitude, and women develop it consciously and carefully in their diaries. This excerpt from a journal by American Louise Mattlage is taken from a larger excerpt published in 1986 in *Women and Aging: An Anthology by Women*:

> Have I said what eighty has to live for? There is so much. The mystery that awaits us is near. Tomorrow is never there. Now is the most marvelous thing in the world. The future is delicious conjecture. And the absolutely sure, unshakable conviction that life is only a part of being. The continuing certainty that the beyond is full of marvelous surprises.

Old women are victims, nonetheless, and their fate, while private, is universal. In this century, they face interment in a retirement home, freedom in a one-room fiefdom, or ignominy in the family home. And, of course, there are two sides to that story: we should not forget their daughters or daughters-in-law who have responsibility for their care if they're incompetent and/or incontinent.

Oddly enough, though, an old woman alone has more freedom than she has ever had in her life. No one is close enough to her to disapprove of her behaviour. No one cares enough to mind what she looks like or what she eats. If she is physically safe — and some old women are not, subject to granny-bashing or street mugging because they're too weak to defend themselves — she can be comfortable in her twilight zone: a disintegrating family home, a cluttered apartment, a tacky room, an indifferent nursing home (less freedom there). If a woman has relatively good health, not counting the usual aches and pains that aging bodies endure, and enough wits to enjoy reading, crossword puzzles, or television and the infrequent visits of family and friends, she can have a "nice life." What she has most of is solitude, and she must learn to make good use of it. If she has paper, she can.

Irish playwright Lady Augusta Gregory feels amply compensated in her age and solitude. "Loneliness," she writes at the age of seventy-six, "made me rich." But it takes practice.

"A notebook might be the very thing for all the old who wave away crossword puzzles, painting, petit point, and knitting. It is more restful than conversation, and for me it has become a companion, more a confessional." This is Florida Scott-Maxwell's solution to age and solitude. Born in Florida, Florida Scott (1883-1979) was an actor at age sixteen, but left the stage when she married John Maxwell. She went to live with him in Scotland, where she reared their children and wrote plays and novels. After her husband's death, she trained as an analytical psychologist, studying under Carl Jung, and then worked in psychological clinics in Scotland and England until her retirement.

In her eighty-second year, she decides to keep a journal principally to explore the phenomenon of being old. During the time she keeps her journal, she undergoes major surgery and finds she is still making discoveries, still encountering emotions in herself that she didn't expect, still caught up in her life. This is the kind of self-recrimination she hurls at herself for expending too much of her limited vigour on her intensity: "I am too frail for moral fervour."

What is most astonishing in Scott-Maxwell is her continuing energy and the joy that permeates the book: "Now that I am sure this freedom is the right garnering of age I am so busy being old that I dread interruptions." She admits, however, "that it takes more courage than I had known to drink the lees of life."

The Measure of My Days presents a challenging example of how to grow old gracefully with a diary as companion and fellow explorer. Scott-Maxwell's vision of life is worth heeding. It's a realistic view: "*Being old* I am out of step, troubled by my lack of concord, unable to like or understand much that I see. Feeling at variance with the times must be the essence of age, and it is confusing, wounding."

Thus she begins her diary. She puts her finger squarely on the problem of age: being "out of step" or "at variance with the times" — being out of sync, we would say today. She wonders: "These endless years before the end, can we summon enough merit to warrant a place for ourselves?"

Deborah Norris Logan did that, too. Although she had trouble with her pens all her life, she kept her diary for twenty-four years until her death at age seventy-eight. When she is seventy-two, she has this to say about growing old:

December 31, 1833
Upon self-examination I do not find that I am one
bit better than I was this day a year ago. And I am
one year older, nearer to eternity, uglier and more
infirm, passing rapidly down the steep of age.

Yet Logan feels compelled to keep on putting something
down on paper, although she admits to taking less pleasure
in it than she did — such folly — but it's a habit by now
that she can't break.

The world closes in, narrower and narrower, until the
perimeters of one's own body are all one has; and yet there
persists the will, some spark, something that asserts, "I write,
therefore I am." Somehow, the act of writing effects a kind
of reconciliation with encroaching age.

Belgian-born American writer May Sarton expresses
the kind of reconciliation required:

June 6, 1982
A face without lines that shows no mark of what
has been lived through in a long life suggests something unlived, empty behind it.... Still, one mourns
one's young face sometimes.

Sarton, a respected and prolific novelist and poet with a
devoted following, published her first diary, *Journal of a
Solitude*, in 1973, following it with five more. Through each
successive journal, she has expressed herself more honestly
and never less than eloquently. She disturbs us with what she
withholds in her first journal and then, as she becomes more
comfortable with the diary form, with her recoveries and

discoveries about her aging, solitary self. More vulnerable in *After the Stroke*, she acknowledges the loneliness of her struggle, hard lines that have nothing to do with those of age:

> August 22, 1986
> [I]f I mind the wrinkles now it is because I have failed to ascend *inside* to what is happening *inside* — and that is a great adventure and challenge, perhaps the greatest in a lifetime — a part of accepting the human condition.

Old women have usually been associated with solitude, not to mention a cat, a broom, and a monologue (that is, they talk to themselves). Statistics Canada reveals that three-quarters of Canadian women spend their last years single: most live with their families — usually daughters; some live in institutions — where they might as well be alone; increasing numbers of them live entirely alone — 40 percent of them below the poverty line. Not that solitude is bad but, like poverty, it takes some getting used to.

Today's old woman may have transmuted her barren isolation into productive loneliness: "Alone but not lonely," as the saying goes. She converses with her diary, where she can maunder and meander and muse and amaze herself. It's safer. As Florida Scott-Maxwell says, "If a grandmother wants to put her foot down, the only safe place to do it these days is in a notebook." She only wishes that a notebook could laugh.

Age sits like time, heavy on her hands and head. It takes

a while for that to happen, however. Inside, most women still feel young. As American writer Gertrude Stein said, "We are always the same age inside." Somehow, the spirit stays frisky.

African-American activist and writer Alice Dunbar-Nelson (1875-1935) testifies to this spirit:

> Tuesday, July 19, 1927
> My birthday! 52 years old. Ye gods! Can you believe it? I feel about 32; looks 42. So that's serene....

She sounds like the young Eva Slawson:

> August 20, 1914
> I am 32 years old today! I can scarcely believe it —
> I certainly don't feel my age. I am sure I felt 32 at
> 22, and 22 at 32! If I go on this way and live to be
> 60, I shall then probably *feel* about 16!

Dunbar-Nelson begins to protest a little as more years pass:

> Thursday, July 19, 1928
> My birthday! Fifty-three today. Feel much younger than when I was 33....

> Friday, July 19, 1919
> My birthday! the 54! and my pen is on the blink!...
> Birthday thoughts? None. I am fifty-four, feel twenty-five, look forty. What will the New Year bring?

French novelist George Sand (1804-1876) in 1869 considered herself more aged than we would today:

... and now I am very old, gently traversing my sixty-fifth year.... My old age is as chaste in thought as it is in deed. I have no regret for youth, no ambition for fame, and no desire for money, except that I would like to have a little to leave to my children and grandchildren. I have no complaints to make of my friends. My one sorrow is that humanity does not go forward fast enough.

My plan in jotting down these thoughts and feelings was based on a theory I once believed in. I used to imagine that I could pick up my own identity from time to time and carry it on. Can one thus resume one's self? Can one know one's self? Is one ever *somebody?* I don't know anything about it any more. It now seems to me that one changes from day to day and that every few years one becomes a new being.

Age is a falling-away time, changing or not, poor or not. Diarists who maintain their writing habit into old age find little things to fuss about as their world narrows, like their scratchy pens. They still have exciting thoughts to think, though, like Florida Scott-Maxwell's: "I feel like a hierarchy, and perhaps I am one. I am my chief interest because to me I am life. My curiosity, delight, pain tell me about life itself."

If she does not outlive her self, if she keeps on going inward and finding more of herself inside, intact, then finally the crone is centred. She is at the peak of her powers. If only others could tap into her strength!

In June 1974, retired American college professor Joyce Mary Horner (1903-1980) fell, breaking several bones. Reduced by this accident to a semi-invalid state aggravated by an increasingly debilitating arthritis and having no one to take care of her, Horner moved into a nursing home. "You've come down on the world," she writes, "down into the world, and what a world — the small world of clocks and routines, wheelchairs and commodes." Determined to use her time well, she keeps a chronicle, at first faithfully, then more and more intermittently, until her discharge in June 1977.

She considers it interesting to "find oneself at this age so activist"; she feels apologetic about pitying herself; she thinks one spends "half one's life in age being ashamed of oneself." She discovers her strength in weakness as she scorns self-pity:

April 2, 1975
I will not write out of self-pity, which I place very
low in the scale of emotions — even nostalgia
ranks higher, its imagery is more varied.

On October 7, 1975, she suggests that nostalgia "takes the place of fantasy" because fantasy "plays a very small part in age, that is, as long as one has one's senses."

An occasional poet, published in *The New Yorker*, Horner brings her sharp senses to bear on the dullness of routine in a nursing home, but is deflected into observing herself and her own reactions. She confronts the dead-end aspect of it as she realizes, "with a wintriness like today's landscape

… that there was nowhere to go from here" (October 30, 1975).

Horner decides that death "loses all terror — or most of it — in a nursing home … this house of continual writing on the wall." She reads May Sarton's novel *As We Are Now*, which is about an old woman in a nursing home, and agrees with the character in her discovery "that nursing homes are purgatory" (December 1976).

Though she began with an outward focus, intending "a-day-in-the-life slice," Horner found to her dismay — but not to ours — that she tended to turn more and more inward. She considered herself trapped in "the prison of self" and found herself unable to find the key. No matter where one is, one takes Self along, and she is not always a pleasant companion.

Horner left the home at the end of the month, for surgery, three years before her death. She made a remarkable discovery in this flat, small, narrow world, and that was her own courage. She is the kind of person one would like to be stranded with on a desert island — or in a nursing home.

Without a careful reading, aging women's unsettling discoveries remain concealed. Younger people tend to avoid the elderly, unless they're doing research. Although eager young historians rummage in the attics for the diaries of great-grandmothers and run around with tape recorders to catch old-timers' tales before it's too late, they still can't seem to hear the whispering voices of the crones. To associate with senior citizens, as they are euphemistically called, is to associate with things one would rather not think about. (If age is there, can death be far behind?) Besides, people want facts and tidbits; they don't want revelations.

Interestingly, many diarists have commented that they dread dying less than aging, and death less than dependence. In age, as Horner discovered, a woman frequently discovers her essential self, the person she has been trying to define all these years. If she's a diarist, she finds that Other Person has been waiting for her all the time, within the pages of her diary. She's reading her own lines and she refuses to be rubbed out.

Many women, of course, do not consciously set out on the quest for self. Many are forced into introspection by life events and by ordeals that shove them onto their uppers and into their interior.

Trying Experiences

ORDEAL N.
1. AN ANCIENT TEUTONIC MODE OF TRIAL, IN WHICH A SUSPECTED PERSON WAS SUBJECT TO SOME PHYSICAL TEST FRAUGHT WITH DANGER.
2. *FIG.* ANYTHING WHICH SEVERELY TESTS CHARACTER OR ENDURANCE; A TRYING EXPERIENCE, A TRIAL.

The Oxford Universal Dictionary

The difference, of course, between hardship and adventure lies in personal choice and freedom. Some women have never had a choice. Those who have left records of ordeals they suffered without choice, have risen to heights of courage and heroism by the manner in which they faced their fate.

There are different kinds of ordeals: those arising out of physical or mental illness, of oneself or a loved one; life-threatening and mind-destroying hazards imposed by war, imprisonment, confinement in a mental institution, or in an abusive relationship; pain and fear inflicted by horrible accidents or vicious people. And then there is death, met any number of ways, including the above, and with encroaching age and frailty.

In the latter half of this century, people tend to publish their tales of ordeals survived. Not all of these accounts are based on diaries. However, the ones with the greatest immediacy are not the "as told to" stories but the "as lived by" ones.

In *A Book of One's Own*, Thomas Mallon reports a touching diary kept on the blank pages of a chequebook, found after a young woman's death from exposure when she was lost in the mountains in Wyoming. A published journal of a somewhat similar circumstance, but with a happier ending, describes events that took place in 1967. Eleanor Dart (b. 1946) backpacked into the mountains in Baja, Mexico, in February with her boyfriend, intending to climb Picacho del Diablo (Devil's Peak) because it was there and because he wanted to. A series of misadventures, bad choices, wrong turnings, inadequate supplies, and separation of the two gradually built up to an ordeal Eleanor doubted at times she would survive. She kept writing in her diary, recording her hallucinations (caused by hunger and pain), and repeating her determination, despite her fears, to stay alive. Her writing in the diary was one way of doing so. She plans to write in the margins when she runs out of paper: "I must write."

At the same time, her father, Francis Dart, who was organizing search attempts, was also keeping a diary. Each of them, beyond the external struggle, was making discoveries. Eleanor:

Sunday, February 26, 1967
Let's talk about religion and faith for a bit. Mine has gone up and down this trip.... Once I have to let go of fighting for my life with my own powers, I find peace and inner strength.

I've read proofs of God's existence and the proofs of the opposite, and I'm sure that there *is* no proof, just this inner peace that comes when "all our strivings cease." That Quaker hymn means a lot to me just now — let go, let go of desires and passions and being fixed on some concrete goal, and let the "still dew of quietness" descend. Find the "beauty of thy peace" even in death. Especially in death, for what else have we to cling to then?

I don't find inner peace too often. I'm too obsessed with striving. But it is there.

Eleanor Dart O'Bryon's diary was published in 1987, interleaved with her father's simultaneous one. She writes a kind of coda to her former self, a refugee from the sixties, and to her father, who died in 1976. She says she never mourned him, but now she doesn't have to. She concludes with a letter he wrote to her in 1971, which echoes what she discovered on that mountain: "We each die continually, almost randomly, one hope at a time. One defeat after another is death enough. But we learn too that no hurt is forever. One recovery at a time, one joy at a time, is resurrection enough."

Psychiatrist Viktor E. Frankl, who survived concentration camp and who made a life study of the phenomenon of survival, observed in his book, *Man's Search for Meaning*, that the very tension generated by the search for the meaning of human existence is itself necessary to mental health. As for the meaning, he quotes Nietzsche: "He who has a *why* to live for can bear almost any *how*."

Women who have endured prison and survived usually had a reason why. Those who kept diaries make it clear, and in fact, sometimes the diary itself becomes the reason why.

On July 12 in 1913 an English suffragette, Gladys Roberts of Leeds, a former solicitor's clerk, was sentenced to one month in Holloway Prison for throwing stones. Her intention and that of her sister suffragettes was to be arrested. She kept a secret journal of her experiences in prison. (This diary is in Dale Spender's book, *Women of Ideas, and What Men Have Done to Them*.)

On the second day, Roberts is removed from her initial cell for breaking window panes and is sentenced to seven days' close confinement. She writes:

[I] was brought down to this cell with nothing in it except a block of wood fixed to the wall for a chair and a plank bed and pillow ... unbreakable opaque windows and double iron doors — God help me stick it! I can hear the others singing, thank goodness!

They have brought us a pint of cocoa and a lump of the usual bread. Hunger strike commences. The drum and fife band is coming at eight o'clock. I wonder if we shall hear it. We seem to be buried alive.

Thursday, July 15

I lie on the bed — I feel so weak — breakfast has just been put in. I said I didn't want any. God help me! I wonder if those outside are thinking about us. I am a coward....

I have seen the doctor.... He said he was very sorry to see us here, and I couldn't keep back a few tears when he had gone. I feel so weak. A wardress brought in a Bible, Prayer Book and Hymn Book. I read the marriage service over. I thought it would get my blood up, so I read Paul's opinion on the duties of a wife.

Gladys Roberts had a cause she believed in and she chose to honour her belief with action. It's more difficult to survive when one begins to question why one bothers. Janina Bauman (b. 1927?) was a teenager in Warsaw, daughter of a well-off middle-class family, when the Germans invaded

Poland. Thrust into the ghetto, Janina somehow survived, living in impossible conditions, barely escaping several times to others more impossible, losing relatives and friends on the way, until 1945 and the end of the war. She scribbled pages of a diary from time to time, losing them, finding more paper, scribbling more. Just before she left Warsaw for the countryside, she stuffed her papers beneath the floorboards of a partially destroyed house. Nine months later, in May 1945, back in Warsaw, she found the house where she had stashed her papers. Still half-ruined, the house was nevertheless occupied. Janina asked for permission to look in the unused, damaged room where she had left her diary; all her copybooks and loose sheets were still there, hidden in the hole in the floor.

Back in 1942, the young woman can make no sense of life:

> November 2
> I keep thinking about people who know what
> they're doing with their lives: people who decide to
> fight an overwhelming military power; people who
> set their hearts on building a better life somewhere
> far away; or those who do the same in their own
> countries by fighting social inequality. I'm none of
> these. I belong nowhere. Have I lived for anything?
> Is there any reason why I should keep running for
> my life?

Two horrible years later, in October 1944, she finds it hard to believe that she is still alive, with her mother and sister and an aunt. She has nightmares, she questions the precarious security they have found in the country, being sheltered by a Catholic family who she believes don't realize they are Jewish. She is affected and infected, she fears, by the Christian faith as she and her family pretend to join in worship with their protectors by attending church and learning the Catechism. She falls in love with a handsome young priest. And then she confronts herself:

> 11 December, 1944
> How can I become a Christian? I don't belong to them, I can't I don't even want to. I belong to the Jews. Not because I was born one or because I share their faith — I never have done. I belong to the Jews because I have suffered as one of them. It's suffering that has made me Jewish.

Her ordeal has taught her who she is.

In 1944, German writer Luise Rinser (b. 1911), a young widow and mother of two children, was denounced by a friend, arrested on a charge of high treason, and imprisoned in the women's prison at Traunstein in Bavaria. She found paper in her cell and kept a diary. Her very first lines, on October 22, 1944, explaining the discovery of the paper and her intention to write, continues: "Writing is strictly prohibited. I am writing nonethcless. The Word mercifully cushions me, coming between me and the naked experience of imprisonment." Thus she invokes Diary as *Word*, buffer not audience. During her confinement, she makes a remarkable discovery:

25 November, 1944
Sometimes in here I confront myself as I have never
done before. I see myself with all my base instincts,
with false, lying, romantic notions of honour,
morality, class-consciousness and all the beautiful,
conventional ideas one acquires. In the end all that
is left is the animal, wanting to eat and sleep, afraid
of being beaten, yearning for freedom. In our lives
outside we simply disguise all of that with a lot
of words.

Shortly before Christmas (December 21, 1944), Rinser is
despairing because of her children, questions her own fear
and despair, and comforts herself. She asks:

Why was I frightened of dying? I haven't been
condemned yet. And what if I had been? For a
moment I felt a deep relief at the thought of death.
... I believe I shall now be able to bear whatever
fate is in store for me.

The very act of recording something in a diary comforts
the writer. She can give herself encouragement or analyze
her pain or promise relief. She can also observe herself and
somehow keep a firmer grasp on things as they should be,
even if they aren't. She becomes both player and audience
and the distancing helps. Every ordeal may not lead to self-
discovery, but recovery is possible.

Marriage has always drawn a curtain over sexual matters, thicker and more opaque and impenetrable than any
silence imposed by prudence or censorship. A woman's

loyalty to her husband and her own sense of pride prevent her from divulging anything that goes on in the conjugal bedroom. This self-imposed silence extends to abuse and battering. Out of loyalty, a woman will excuse her husband's violence, putting it down to frustration, weariness, anxiety for her and the children, or she will deny his cruelty out of equal parts pride and guilt: too proud to admit she has been subject to such treatment, and guilty because she feels she must be responsible for it. Until this century, her husband's treatment of her has remained a matter between the diarist and her diary and even then she doesn't tell all: it's "a secret to be burried."

Iowa-born Martha van Orsdol Shaw Farnsworth (1867–1924) moved to Kansas when she was five and lived there the rest of her life, except for a brief foray to California with her tubercular first husband for reasons of his health. She began her first diary when she was fourteen and kept it for forty years. The journal is her closest friend and only confidante during her stormy first marriage. She prays on her wedding day, September 4, 1889, for God's blessing — and she will need it. Her husband had a problem with liquor and his temper. Early on, Martha writes that while her heart is full of sorrow, yet she smiles "happily," though she feels "the opposite." By November 4, 1892, she spells out her feelings and her decision:

Johnny is so abusive, he has driven from my heart all love for him, and he does not *dream* that his cruelty has killed my heart and it cannot love him. I would be so glad of my freedom.... I stay with him,

simply because, I believe as a Christian, it is my
duty to do so. I do not believe in divorces.

Fearing that she has been guilty of self-pity, she feels justified when she cites her brother-in-law as witness to her
troubles:

> August 31, 1893
> Johnny is so ill-natured and abusive to me, that his
> brother goes after him, sometimes and "*hushes him
> up*," telling him, he ought to be ashamed of himself
> for abusing one, who has done so much for him
> and does all in her *power* for him, day after day,
> uncomplainingly.

Johnny Shaw died on October 26, 1893. Martha put some
things away and burned more, wanting no reminder of her
marriage. She buried her wedding veil and gloves with her
husband. On November 2 Martha wrote,

> I feel as if a great load had been lifted from off me
> and my freedom is actually a joy, tho' I sincerely
> grieve, that death should be the means of this thrill
> of pleasure, at being free from such a miserable life.

Women still mask their pain and hide their bruises, stick
by their men out of loyalty and die-hard faith, and claim
their sanity by calling witness in the private pages of a
diary, but they don't leave, and they don't tell anyone. A
diary is a beginning, the beginning of telling.

Diarists have remained silent about abuse until this century. Only recently have sexual abuse, wife battering, and

incest emerged in women's journals as, not tales to be told, but trauma to be dealt with. Elly Danica (b. 1947) wrote *Don't: A Woman's Word* in the present tense, in a diary form, as a memory that must be reclaimed before she can live in the present.

"It's now or never," she writes. "I learn to live with never. Never again. I don't remember. I don't want to remember. Memory pursues me. Memory uses a pen to pursue me." Memories can't save anyone but sometimes they can help to heal.

A diary can't save a woman from mental illness any more than it can stop a beating or hold back death. What diaries do show us of women who have suffered depression or neurosis is how uncrazy they are. In the past, "madness" has often been a convenient tag for discontented women, the ones who could see the bars of their cage with no hope of escape. Before divorce became easier, a man could put his wife in a mental asylum; it was cheaper and even more effective than divorce.

American psychologist Phyllis Chesler points out that "most women who are psychiatrically hospitalized are not 'mad'.... They are depressed, suicidal, frigid, anxious, paranoid, phobic, guilty, indecisive, inactive, and without hope." But not mad.

In her book, *Women and Madness*, Chesler lists four women who were put in asylums: Elizabeth Packard (1816-c. 1890); Ellen West (c. 1890-c. 1926); Zelda Fitzgerald (1900-1948); and Sylvia Plath. Three of these women kept diaries.

In 1860, Elizabeth Packard's husband had her committed to a private hospital for the insane, which she always called a prison, for daring to have her own opinions about religious freedom. The first to compare institutional psychiatry with the Inquisition, Packard kept a secret diary of what happened to her and other female inmates. After she "escaped," she published two books, one of which, *Modern Persecution or Insane Asylums Unveiled* (1873), was based on her asylum journal. This and *The Liabilities of the Married Women* were her only source of earnings because her husband had confiscated her inherited income.

Ellen West's story is written up as a case history by Ludwig Binswanger in Rollo May's *Existence*. Rebellious and a poet, West was among the first diagnosed anorexics. (*The Oxford English Dictionary* dates the first use of the term *anorexia* at 1873.)

"Something in me rebels against becoming fat," West writes in her diary and questions her own temperament: "For what purpose did nature give me health and ambition? ... [I]t is really sad that I must translate all this force and urge to action into unheard words [in her diary], instead of powerful deeds.... I am twenty-one years old and am supposed to be silent and grin like a puppet. I am no puppet. I am a human being with red blood and a woman with quivering heart...."

Sylvia Plath's novel *The Bell Jar* (1963) is based on her own breakdown when she was hospitalized as she struggled with her demons. Her metaphor of the bell jar is adumbrated by West: "I feel myself excluded from all real life. I am quite isolated. I sit in a glass ball. I see people through a glass wall.... [M]y hands merely beat against the walls of my glass ball."

What Plath faced was the either/or impasse frequently confronted by a woman writer who has difficulty choosing between the traditional role of wife and mother and her personal drive for creation. With two children and separated from her husband, the successful poet Ted Hughes, Plath wrote what is considered to be her masterpiece, *Ariel*, in October 1962, towards the end of her life. She committed suicide in February 1963 at the age of thirty-one.

In July 1957, married for a year, Plath thinks she hears the doors of her prison swinging shut:

> I have never in my life, except that deadly summer of 1953, & fall [when she had her breakdown], gone through such a black lethal two weeks. I couldn't write a word about it, though I did in my head. The horror, day by day more sure, of being pregnant. Remembering my growing casualness about contraception, as if it couldn't happen to me then: clang, clang, one door after another banged shut with the overhanging terror which, I know now, would end me.... Nothing, till Monday, when, after a busy, deceptive morning of shopping, I sat at the typewriter and the hot drench itself began, the red stain dreamed of and longed for during the white sterile ominous minutes of the six weeks.

She had a push-me-pull-you attitude. By January 1958, she writes:

> I want one [a baby].... Four years of marriage child-
> less is enough for us? Yes, I think I shall have guts
> by then.

She goes on:

> June 20, 1958
> I have even longed for that most fearsome first
> woman's ordeal: having a baby — to elude my
> demanding demons and have a constant excuse for
> lack of production in writing.

She had two poems accepted by *The New Yorker*, which sent her into a productive phase, but not without its trauma:

> July 7, 1958
> I am evidently going through a stage in beginning
> writing similar to my two months of hysteria in
> beginning teaching last fall. A sickness, frenzy of
> resentment at everything but myself at the bottom.
> I lie wakeful at night, wake exhausted with that
> sense of razor-shaved nerves. I must be my own
> doctor.

Women must nurture themselves. Sometimes, but not always, a diary can save them. Note that Plath realizes her need of nurturing, but then she accuses herself of hysteria.

Hysteria is a distinctively female complaint, deriving from the Greek *hustera*, "womb." Freud saw women as "cranky children with uteruses" and treated them accordingly. Neurasthenia was another favourite label to stick on women before and after the turn of this century, a convenient designation meaning the doctor didn't know what was wrong. Diarist Eva Slawson died of undiagnosed diabetes tagged neurasthenia by her doctor. She had been suffering with pains in her legs for some time:

November 3, 1914
I feel rather anxious about the nerves of my legs — they pain me so — I get depressed about it all, and today have been more than usually conscious of discomfort.

November 26, 1914
I tossed the hours away, the nerves of my legs aching, and sad thoughts flitting through my mind.

November 27
This has been a day of depression — it has been difficult to feel the beauty and wonder of life, and light and love have seemed far off. On my way home this evening, I upbraided myself — I recalled my richness....

February 22, 1915
Dr. Shone's advice to me, "a complete change of life," as a cure for neurasthenia, has been very much in my mind today, making me scheme and plan for the future.

Inevitably, diarists must face their own death. If anything, New England spinster Alice James received the news of her imminent death with something like relief. She had been an invalid all her life, her symptoms largely undiagnosed. At last she has something real wrong with her, something to die of! She writes:

June 1st, 1891
To any one who has not been there, it will be hard to understand the enormous relief of Sir A.C.'s [her doctor] uncompromising verdict, lifting us out of the formless vague and setting us within the very heart of the sustaining concrete. One would naturally not choose such an ugly and gruesome method of progression down the dark Valley of the Shadow of Death and of course many of the moral sinews will snap by the way, but we shall gird up our loins and the blessed peace of the end will have no shadow cast upon it.

Then James schools herself to the thought of leaving:

June 24th
Half a dozen times a day I find myself saying, "I must ask K about that," or "I must find out about this," with the idea that some day I may need the knowledge, when suddenly I am stopped off by the thought that the "some days" are over for me; a thought natural and simple, and of a most desirable complexion. It seems more like the gentle dropping of natural things, than the taking up of spiritual ones; as it comes nearer, it will doubtless seem more positive.

Marie Lénéru, who was crippled, blind, and deaf from the age of thirteen, puts a different spin on it:

> December 13, 1902
> We are less poor through what we lose, than through what we have missed, and less thwarted by what we have no longer than by what we shall never have.

How good it is to have a diary, a private place in which one can speak of suffering, as Lénéru does:

> September 9, 1899
> ... Suffering is a degradation. We make an absurd merit of our "having suffered," since necessity assumes exclusive responsibility for accomplishing this.

Different diarists come to different conclusions about suffering. Poor sick Katherine Mansfield has obviously given it a lot of thought:

> 18 October, 1920
> ... [S]uffering, bodily suffering such as I've known for three years ... has changed for ever everything — even the *appearance* of the world is not the same — there is something added. *Everything has its shadow*.... I feel it has been an immense privilege. Yes, in spite of all. How blind we little creatures are! ... [I]t's only the fairy tales we *really* live by....
> I believe the greatest failing of all is *to be*

frightened. Perfect Love casteth out Fear. When I look back on my life all my mistakes have been because I was afraid.... Was that why I had to look on death? Would nothing less cure me? You know, one can't help wondering sometimes.... No, not a personal God or any such nonsense. Much more likely — the soul's desperate choice.

Etty Hillesum (1941-1943), a Dutch Jew who took amazing spiritual as well as physical risks, kept her diaries from 1941 to 1943, her last entry made in Westerbork before she was taken with her family to Auschwitz to die. Realizing she is "tightly wound as a ball of twine," she begins searching for what she calls a little "mental hygiene." She records a spiritual growth that staggers the heart as she takes constant risks with her health and sanity. Having lost track of date and time in Westerbork, Hillesum writes early one morning:

> I have been lying here trying to assimilate just a little of the terrible suffering that has to be endured all over the world.... Today will be a hard day. I shall lie quietly and try to "anticipate" something of all the hard days that are to come.
>
> When I suffer for the vulnerable is it not for my own vulnerability that I really suffer?...
>
> We should be willing to act as a balm for all wounds.

This final entry causes the earth to open beneath her readers' feet.

When English writer Barbara Pym was diagnosed with cancer, she becomes curiously detached about her coming ordeal:

13 January, 1979
How did people die in the old days (not the 19th century but really old days like the 17th century). What did they do about cancer? If I'd been born in 1613 I would have died in 1671. I'd certainly have been dead in 1674.

As for the suffering involved, she writes:

5 August
Perhaps what one fears about dying won't be the actual moment — one hopes — but what you have to go through beforehand — in my case this uncomfortable swollen body and feeling sick and no interest in food or drink.

By the last entry in her diary, Pym has become so detached, she has clearly cut her threads:

21 November
The curious mixed or unisex ward is surely Donne's:

> Difference of sex no more we know
> Than our guardian angels do.

She died on January 11, 1980.

Little by little, female diarists finally began to notice

what Carol Gilligan in her book *A Different Voice* has called "their own exclusion of themselves." Some glimmer of recognition begins to filter through when they face death. A shaft of light illuminates their understanding perhaps for the first time. All their lives most women have been living someone else's script, speaking in someone else's voice, seeing themselves through someone else's eyes, never their own. In death the scales finally fall from their dimming eyes and the voice they have been attempting to find murmurs revolution. It's just a murmur.

CHAPTER FIVE

Reading Between the Lines

IT DOES NOT REQUIRE A GREAT LEAP OF
IMAGINATION FOR A WOMEN TO UNDER-
STAND THE FEMININE PRINCIPLE AS A
GRAND COLLECTION OF COMPROMISES,
LARGE AND SMALL, THAT SHE SIMPLY MUST
MAKE IN ORDER TO RENDER HERSELF A
SUCCESSFUL WOMAN.

Susan Brownmiller

If a woman is forced by circumstances beyond her control to confront herself, if travel changes her perspective or adventure her attitude, if age gives her the courage and impunity to take a long look at a life that she could do nothing about by that time, or if anguish drags her to the edge of an abyss she never wanted to look into, then, only then (and not always), might she begin to acknowledge some insights into her inner life and self.

It's easier but lonelier for the mavericks to find their way to the inner landscape. The "safe" ones, the ones who seem never to be alone, can't afford to withdraw their investment in their life's work. Where would they go? What would they do? Who would they be? And what would they say? So they stay where they are, say nothing and keep on working, coping with daily life and accepting their lot. They enter their daily code, hoping to make sense of it all — or not — and apparently not discovering or changing much.

Traumatic events raise questions most diarists would sooner not ask if they could avoid it. That way lies anarchy and discontent and anger. When a bad thing happens, when the pain is too great, they silence themselves. The words they use mask feeling. They resign themselves in their diaries.

Thy Will Be Done

ALL THINGS WORK TOGETHER FOR GOOD TO
THEM THAT LOVE GOD.

Romans 8: 28

Until very recently, most women led generic, no-frills lives, with no intention or comprehension, or the slightest possibility of determining their own destiny. If in her diary a woman even begins to question the unfairness of her lot, if she acknowledges that perhaps she's less than thrilled with what she's been dealt, she quickly backtracks with a *but*. Always, always, the second half of the sentence is *but*: but — I'm not complaining; but — all will be well; but — Thy will be done; but — I'll try to understand and if I can't understand I'll try to accept; but — see — I'm trying to make the best of it; but—out of this evil some good will come; but — for God's sake, as Mary Chesnut says, *have pity!!*

There is a kind of automatic smoothing over, nervous and reflexive, like hands smoothing out a towel or a skirt. When Emily Gillespie reports bad news or hard times in her own life or others, she always concludes with a little homily, almost by rote, to deny it, to soothe it all away. Thus, when she leaves her home and family to visit and work for an aunt and uncle in Iowa, she writes:

> ... ah, true tis a life *journey* and may it be for the
> best, but, ah the trial to leave parents & friends, to
> live far away, but, I trust that all may yet be well.

And on the eve of her marriage, she leans on her now ritual, soothing formula: "— but may I trust that all will be well, that the will of God be done."

She repeats that litany, *all is well*, or some variation of it, throughout her diary, after any report of disaster and usually at the conclusion of a year or a diary, the physical book she writes in.

Other guilty, self-conscious, tongue-tied or pen-swoggled women also fall back — heavily — on ritual and litany, and on handy clichés, mouthing stock phrases that have nothing to do with how they really feel. They use them as fillers to cover discontent, wonder, confusion, or rage. The string of clichés, old saws, tired maxims, and sampler philosophy could be written by anyone — Anonymous, who Virginia Woolf said was probably a woman.

Canadian doctor Elizabeth Smith learned her little incantations early in life. Even as a nineteen-year-old schoolteacher in Speyside, Ontario, she had a forewarning of the double standard in the treatment of men and women that she was to suffer from later. She confesses to her diary on June 17, 1878, that she was "very wrothy at the idea that when Andrew P was successful [in the exams for medical school] after the poor answering he made that I should be so used because I was a girl, not a boy forsooth!" She goes on to conjecture that if she were a boy, she might even be made superintendent of the Sunday school she started, but then, like most women, she tries to deflect her anger and comforts herself:

> As I view the fields the hills trees & valleys the homesteads and far away blue sky from my school-room door I cannot but be less stern, less rebellious to the things of life as I find them. They are great softeners of surly mood.

Smith fell back on her arsenal of comforting bromides later in her life when she had good reason for despair and anger. Like most of the other faithful diarists, she invokes God's assistance and grace, gives constant thanks for all her blessings, and during the very hardest time, when she is struggling against the prejudice and vituperation of her male professors and colleagues, she still acknowledges the source of her strength and ultimate deliverance:

> December 14, 1882
> It all seems like a horrible dream from wh. I must awaken but yet has been long & terrible. Then too the weight of it must hand [*sic*] over us all through this usually merry time, this time of Peace &

Goodwill to Men, & yet I feel today that in God's good time out of this evil good *will* come, somehow somewhere, sometimes, "good will be the final goal of ill" I pray Heaven it may be so, for now it is very dark.

Most diarists echo this familiar litany, a parroting of prayers they have been taught, with bits of the scripture thrown in. This habit probably goes all the way back to when the diary was a daily devotional in written form (in other words, a task). It became a habit that dies hard: diary as prayer, another task to be performed, a mental laying-on of hands — a blessing. When a diarist writes such a prayer, this plea to a higher authority is usually at the end of her entry. Prayers come in different sizes and with different emotions, depending on the diarist's suffering and on her era. Women from an earlier time seem to have surrendered wholeheartedly to Divine Will. As diarists move forward in time, they take longer to submit: they're reluctant, forgetful, resentful, and finally, almost insincere, as if they were paying mere lip service because it's an unavoidable task, the right thing to do, or maybe even good luck, like throwing salt over your left shoulder if you spill some, or saying "bread-and-butter" when an obstacle separates you from your companion. The performance of the task, that is, the prayer itself, has little or no meaning. The litany provides less and less reassurance, less and less comfort.

Aging women in every generation have given themselves similar advice. Many of them cling to the Word they invested their lives in, that is, the will of the Lord, the faith of their fathers and the submission of their mothers, with the promise of better things in the next life. The Word is reduced in their journals almost to one-liners, slogans, samplers-for-the-living. And all the while they grow older, alone.

On December 13, 1919, just thirteen days past her forty-fifth birthday when she cheered herself by commenting on her own still-dark hair and lack of wrinkles, writer Lucy Maud Montgomery sounds depressed on a "dull gray lifeless day ... without a gleam of sunshine without or within." She confesses to being lonely, starved for companionship for the previous eight weeks with no help from her husband, Ewan, who was ill.

"So I'm utterly alone," she writes, "and once in a while, when a dull, lifeless twilight is wrapping itself over a dull lifeless gray world I give up in a sort of despair and mutter, 'I *can't* go on.'

"But my givings-up never last very long. When I get rested and cheered up by a bit of a dip into some interesting book — or even by a dose of confession in this, my diary — I rise up again and resolve to endure to the end. This little outburst here has quite refreshed me."

It didn't, though. The hard, cold winter dragged on, and Montgomery with it. She was a driven woman, driven by her muse and by her need for acceptance. "At heart," she writes on December 11 a year later, "I am still the snubbed little girl of years ago who was constantly made to feel by all the grown-up denizens of her small world that she was of no importance whatever to any living creature. The impression made on me then can never be effaced — I can never lose my 'inferiority complex.' That little girl can never believe in the reality of any demonstration in her honour. Well, perhaps it is just as well. Likely it is very effective in keeping me from *developing symptoms of swelled head*."

Perhaps it's just as well. Pollyanna used to be every woman's middle name and the Glad Game a prerequisite. What's interesting is that the inner voice of even a successful woman should be so needy and so uncertain of herself. Many women diarists, it seems, needed constant bolstering and support, and if they didn't get it from the people closest to them, they sought it from themselves, in the pages of a diary.

Self-castigation and, rarely, self-absolution follow any self-exposure of bad behaviour. A self-administered scolding and a promise to do better in the future are often accompanied by the comforting placebo of a panacea: "All will be well" (Gillespie), "God's will be done" (Le Guin), "Count your blessings" (most of them). The little girls who begin with a solemn resolve to be better usually go on in the way they were trained, with God's or someone's help. If a diarist can resign herself to see a design in the scheme, her life is not meaningless, hence her reliance on reassuring ritual, a ritual she frequently enshrines in her diary. It takes years of training.

Mary Smith (1864-1945), a Quaker from Philadelphia, married English Catholic Frank Costelloe in 1885 and bore him two daughters. A journal entry in December 1889 indicates how she feels about marriage:

In the present order of things (perhaps it will
always be so) in marriage the man takes everything
from the woman. Of course he gives some things
in exchange, but not all.

He absorbs *the whole* woman's life and gives her
love, support, a home, much of his time, but not his
life, in the sense in which she gives hers....

Her pursuits, *where they do not naturally coincide
with his*, are set aside....

I am told that I shall find my *true* development
in casting myself generously, unreservedly into the
march of his life. This, he says, is what the *union* of
marriage means. (These two shall be one creature
— and that one the husband.) ...

Therefore, woman, sink thyself and thy needs
and empty hopes. They cannot be fulfilled. Join the
army of those who exist to fill up the gaps in the
interesting lives of others and learn, as most women
learn, to consider it enough interest for thee.

Given the trouble she had accepting these ideas, it's not surprising that she left that husband (and her daughters) for another man, becoming on her first husband's death, the wife of the American art critic Bernard Berenson.

How well do ritual phrases serve to tamp down rage? The diarists who comfort themselves with their pat phrases only succeed in masking their anger.

A Terrible Hurdle

THE EXPRESSION OF ANGER HAS ALWAYS BEEN
A TERRIBLE HURDLE IN WOMEN'S PERSONAL
PROGRESS.

Carolyn Heilbrun

Psychiatrist R.D. Laing has said that we all live our lives carrying out post-hypnotic suggestions left over from our childhood; the idea comes as no surprise to women. For centuries, they have functioned under these post-hypnotic commands: be nice, be good, be happy, be a lady, be polite; love, honour, and obey; don't think, don't talk, don't complain, don't cry; shut your eyes, spread your legs, bear up, bear down, smile! Their diaries, in enabling women finally to open their eyes to their own lives, to think, to express their thoughts, and to recognize the difference between fantasy and reality, between what they have been told and what is actually true for them, weaken the bonds of post-hypnosis.

Blessed are the peacekeepers, we are told, for they shall find peace. Women have never been allowed to be anything but peacekeepers. It's not nice to get angry. The trouble is that the nicer they are and the more they are nice, the more they build up an accumulation of anger and rage. American writer Le Anne Schreiber, who published her diary about her mother's terminal illness in 1990 (*Midstream*), claims that her mother had never laid a guilt trip on her, though that had not prevented her from feeling guilty. As Schreiber struggles with her anger at the imminent loss of her mother, she finds she has no tools to fight the marshmallow wall of her family's denial:

Wednesday, October 1, 1986
The rage I had felt this morning flared up to full heat, and I decided to leave the house rather than risk explosion. I am paying the price now for a lifetime of not challenging the family ethic of keeping the peace at all costs.... How can I bring anger into this home, to parents who have barricaded the door against it for as long as I can remember? How can I raise my voice against my mother who is sick and dying, my father strained beyond his understanding?

American psychotherapist Dr. Harriet Goldhor Lerner, in her best-selling book, *The Dance of Anger*, points out that anger is a signal of something else going on, but that the taboos against it are so strong that "even *knowing* when we are angry is not a simple matter," especially for women, especially in the past.

In the past, women were well-schooled, even diarists, even within the relative safety of their private pages. They state the problem, their fear, anxiety, anger — and then resort to their classic *but*-ritual or *and*. ("And I am truly blessed and all things work together for good.") Both *but* and *and* trigger a conditioned reflex. Their lessons have been heavily imposed and carefully taught according to the patriarchal party line. They have learned to adopt a relentlessly, mindlessly, numbingly optimistic attitude to enable them to bear the whips, scorns, and contumelies of life. Even their diaries are not completely safe because some other eyes might see, including their own.

This is an agonizing discovery a diarist would rather not make: the unexpected swelling, crashing tidal waves of rage. Even in the centuries before this outspoken one, the anger is there, hidden between the lines on the page. Sometimes, suddenly the scales fall from her eyes and she sees more clearly than she has ever done. Thus, Mary Chesnut's realization:

> March 4, 1861
> I saw today a sale of Negroes — Mulatto women in *silk dresses* — one girl was on the stand. Nice looking ... she looked as coy & pleased at the bidder. South Carolina slave holder as I am my very soul sickened — it is too dreadful. I tried to reason — this is not worse than the willing sale most women make of themselves in marriage — nor can the consequences be worse. The Bible authorizes marriage & slavery — poor women! poor slaves!

Hotheaded as she is, Chesnut is smart enough to spew her impatience into her diary and spare herself others' anger with her: "How *dare* men mix up the Bible so with their own *bad* passions," she writes, but does not speak it. A wise woman knows when to hold her tongue, or quickly learns.

It took a crucible of rage to force Elizabeth Smith out of the copybook platitudes of her younger days into her own syntax. At medical school this woman went through what she calls "a furnace fiery & severe as any could be" and continues, "Not a day not a lecture passes at Med Coll but something makes me shrink something hurts me, hurts me cruelly, & why? Not because there is anything in the whole range of medicine that should make me blush or feel hurt in the tenderest part of a woman's nature. It is not that, oh no ... but the current through the class of whisper — derisive ... ejaculations, turning what never was meant as unseemly to horrible meanings, the thousand & one ways that can be devised by the foul hearted to create a smile on the faces of their fellows. No one else but those who endure can ever understand how many ways are possible or how day by day it seems harder to bear for we have borne so much.

"And then to know they — *they dare* to judge me immodest, indelicate, unwomanly.... [I]f ever there was a huge injustice crying for redress it is this."

Even when masked, rage never ceases. Michelle Harrison graduated from medical school in 1967. When she was thirty-five, she left teaching and family practice to train in obstetrics and gynaecology at an American hospital. She ran head on against a system that appalled her. Observing that male doctors had turned childbirth into a surgical procedure, she tells her tape recorder, which she uses as a diary, that to these doctors "the medical birth is pornographic" — a sacred, natural act turned ugly. In her confrontations with her superiors, however, she understands that she has to play the game their way or get out. So she tries to bide her time until she has gained the experience she needs.

One day she reports an incident having nothing to do with medicine:

Friday, Day 33

After surgery Carol and I were standing out at the OR desk when Dr. Carter came by to say he was leaving town. Then he leaned over and gave me a pinch on the ass as he left. Containing my rage, I smiled and said, "Have a good trip." Carol and I joked at his having no idea who I really am or how I feel. I was glad to be "in" and accepted, but furious at what that seemed to take.

Until recently, the only safe place to report sexual harassment was in a diary. Is it much safer now?

English writer Barbara Pym, of the quiet humour and ironic aphorism, admits her rage with a man, but only to herself and only once:

May 24, 1965

Fortunately all the fury and bitterness I sometimes feel has stayed hidden inside me and R. doesn't — perhaps never will — know!

If there is any credibility to the idea that repressed emotions of various kinds and unrelieved stress are contributing factors to cancer, then here is another case history. Pym was disappointed in love and never married. After four of her novels had been published, her work was rejected and only "discovered" too late in her life to do much good. Was her cancer Pym's way of expressing her fiery resentment?

In earlier times, female complaints sound, even to themselves, like resentment, whining, griping, bitching — dreaded word! — and the diarists try to stifle them. At least a diary gives a woman a chance to give vent to her real feelings — sometimes — disguised, softened, soothed, rationalized away as they may be.

First, of course, a diarist has to forgive herself. A diary may enable her to do that without taking the blame but simply accepting the consequences. American sculptor Anne Truitt reminds herself how to do this:

June, 1978

I try to consider my mistakes with the tenderness I would bring to bear on those of other people. In doing so, I notice that understanding leads to tempered self-forgiveness because my motivation, shorn of the incidental, seems to have constituted self-preservation. I have come to this position slowly, and with a lot of careful thought, because my instinctive reaction to any failure to meet my own standards is to blame myself mercilessly.

In another diary, Truitt offers another reminder: "It takes kindness to forgive oneself for one's life."

The cracks in the façade do keep appearing and the questions do keep arising. The "I" begins to intrude. The "I" commands a verb, encounters an object, presumes the right. For the first time, "I" becomes the subject of the discussion. This is not to say that the diarist instantly gains any high opinion of herself. She has been too well trained in the ritual of self-censoring, self-effacing, and self-sacrificing for that. But she makes a few discoveries as she allows herself to be more self-indulgent. She begins to divide herself between the outer person who deals with the world and the inner person she faces in her diary.

Even in this century, a diarist has to find her expression without breaking down, she has to find a level tone without self-pity or hysteria, with enough self-discipline to tell herself the truth about herself. She can spare herself some pain if she can find an external object for her attention — a thing, sometimes another person — at any rate, something outside herself that she can focus her emotion on — in short, a metaphor.

The Metaphors of Self

THE SELF EXPRESSES ITSELF BY THE
METAPHORS IT CREATES AND PROJECTS.

James Olney

A room of one's own. To Virginia Woolf — and her class and her profession — the room is a metaphor for women's intellectual autonomy. For women of other classes and education, for women of other countries and centuries, a room of one's own, or at least some kind of private space, is a symbol of survival. The wife/helpmeet, mother/nurturer, at everyone's service but her own, no matter what her class, finds her greatest obstacles to be a lack of privacy and a lack of time to herself.

Alone at last, the diarist writes, with a deep sigh and often with an apology for having let days go by without sitting down to write. As she writes, if she is a mother, it becomes apparent that she is not alone, for she will comment on a little one's activity around her that makes consecutive thought and effort more difficult. The sigh, the apology, the patience, or lack of, are then followed by some breath of gratitude for comparative solitude, with a dollop of time and a pinch of energy enough to put her thoughts — if indeed they be thoughts — at any rate, her account on paper. The interruptions are usually children, though sometimes a husband comes home early. This oasis of time becomes an intangible metaphor, the symbol of a diarist's momentary freedom.

The *room* she writes in is a metaphor of her life. Women have lived out their lives in private rooms, more so than men, whose arena has been outside and more public. A sixteenth-century English proverb defined woman in terms of the rooms she occupied: "a shrew in the kitchen, a saint in the church, an angel at the board, and an ape in the bed." It bears out the association of women within doors. The nineteenth-century expression "angel in the house," coined by an early feminist writer, American Margaret Fuller, repeated with reverence by Henry James, referring to his own mother, and satirized by Woolf, perpetuates the idea of woman's physical placement in the home as guardian of the household. Flitting, hovering, ethereal, the angel exercises no real power. The various rooms in the cliché define her duties as the rooms themselves become both metaphor and prison: kitchen, church (outside the house, but not very public), dining room, bedroom. Add nursery. Home is the nursery for both children and husband and she is the ultimate caregiver.

Though women have been confined to their rooms, their gardens have been their own creations. A woman's garden is a beautiful metaphor, recalling the most powerful female myth, that of Demeter and Kore (Persephone). Reclaimed by her mother from Hades, Kore returns each year from the underworld and asserts renewed life as the seeds burst afresh and the earth blossoms.

New England midwife Martha Ballard reports her annual labour over her garden, as do many of the pioneer women in the West, once they stopped moving, who worked their gardens to feed their families and to nourish their own need for beauty. All of them take pride in their achievement. It wasn't easy for them as they added hoeing and weeding and watering and carrying water to all their other chores.

Flowers were a powerful metaphor in the harsh winters in Dakota Territory. On January 14, 1887, Mary Dodge Woodward, bothered with a frozen finger, reports that the blessed thermometer had finally registered above zero the day before "and even the chickens came and crowed in glee." She goes on to describe her houseplants: "I have a cluster of fuchsias just opening, and how exquisite they look to us here, in this wintry gloom." Later that spring, on March 23 ("Just zero at seven"), the diarist indulges herself in a touch of homesickness for Wisconsin:

> I suppose at home my dooryard is already showing
> the swelling of buds, and perhaps the tulips are
> peeping out, but Dakota is bare. There must be
> hundreds of children in this territory who have
> never seen an apple blossom, and what is worse, I

fear they never will. The absence of such things takes all the poetry out of life.

Garden diaries represent a whole sub-field of lifewriting. The garden with its flowers and care becomes a metaphor for the life of the gardener. American Celia Thaxter (1835-1894) logs her garden with sensuous delight. Towards the end of a September, she offers a sensuous appreciation of her glowing garden in words that could be arranged into found poetry. Herewith a sample only:

> Still the Sweet Peas
> blossom as if
> their thick ranks were ready
> to fly away
> with myriad wings
> of delicious pink,
> blue,
> purple,
> red,
> and white.
> Poppies yet bloom
> Rose Campions at their brightest,
> hemmed in
> with the Scarlet Flax,
> and the stars and suns
> of Marigolds blaze
> with a matchless glory.

Hilda Murrell (1906-1984), English rose grower, widely known to the British public after her unsolved murder, kept personal journals, garden diaries, and planting logs. The published selections of her natural history diaries read like ordinary travel accounts, but are enriched suddenly with a botanist's precise detail, including the Latin names for the flora she described, and with a poet's zeal for recording beauty. Murrell made an excursion to Anglesey in late June of 1981, ending on July 2 with a jaunt to Pen-lôn [*sic*] to look at willows. "Willows," she writes, "are of course dioecious....

"There was an hour of bliss before I had to leave — the warmth of the sun, the *silence*. The sough of the wind in the dune-grass, the small hum of a bee, the quicker whizz of a fly, do not break the silence; they add to it the throb of life and the sense of its miraculous power."

Any writer who gardens puts flowers and nature in her diary, and May Sarton is no exception. Her six published journals record her efforts and her pleasure in her garden:

> April 30, 1983
> My cup runneth over I am so happy to be home
> again and to find the daffodils startling the eye all
> over the field and down the orchard path in all
> their brilliance.

Dorothy Wordsworth (1771-1855) has been credited with being her brother William's eye because she took time in her diary to describe the daffodils in the woods beyond Gowbarrow Park:

> Thursday 15 April, 1802
> I never saw daffodils so beautiful they grew among

the mossy stones about and about them, some rested their heads upon these stones as on a pillow for
weariness and the rest tossed and reeled and danced
and seemed as if they verily laughed with the wind
that blew upon them over the lake, they looked so
gay ever glancing ever changing.

In addition to flowers, other potent images abound among
the diarists. All the recalcitrant pens about which so many
diarists complain, are they metaphors of the stopped-up,
blunted, scratchy feelings, which can never be adequately
expressed?

On the other hand, consider wood piles. During the
winter of 1804, Martha Ballard had a running battle with
her son about her wood supply. Her husband was in jail for
debt and she was alone, dependent on a tired, resentful
daughter-in-law and her busy, belligerent son Jonathan.
Martha could chop and carry, but she couldn't cut and haul
logs; she reports "fatague" over and over again as she tried
to find and gather wood for her heating and baking:

October 24, 1804
Rainy. I have had to go thro the wet to feed my
hoggs, milk my cow, and pique my wood from the
old loggs in the Gardin.

October 25
Clear I have been getting wood and fatagues much
to do. I broke old loggs with an old hough and
brot in the pieces in a baskett and O how fatagued
I was.

October 26
Clear part of the day. I have been giting wood and
finishing my wash that I began last night after 9
hour Evng. Son Jonathans wife here to spin thread.
I Brot a Burthen of Bark after sun sett which took
me 300 & 50 steps. O that I might be patient.

Laurel Ulrich Thatcher, Ballard's historian, points out that
the diarist caused her own problems: the difficulty wasn't
wood but Martha's relationship with her son. The wood was
a metaphor for the warm sympathy and support the woman
needed and wasn't receiving.

Wood piles were important, a symbol of survival.
Canadian pioneer Anne Langton spends an inordinate
amount of diary- and mind-time on her wood supply:

January, 1839
Firing is a most troublesome part of housekeeping
in this country, the drawing-in and cutting up of
wood is endless. It is astonishing to see the piles
that disappear in a day, but it must be so in such a
climate as ours.

As Mary Dodge Woodward commented in her diary,
"There is nothing more handsome than a nice wood pile"
— and all it stands for.

Thus a diarist will focus on an important object in her
life until it becomes a symbol of her self. Margaret
Fountaine, the diarist who bequeathed her butterflies and
locked diaries to the Castle Museum at Norwich, certainly found an apt metaphor for herself.

In March 1894, she found Majola, Italy, to be a "splendid locality for butterflies; the entire female population of *P. Napi* was represented by var. *Vryonia*. Directly I saw the males on the wing I conjectured that at this elevation the female would most probably be of this variety and I was glad to find that I had conjectured rightly; it seems so brutal to rob them of all their little dusky wives and the mothers of the next brood, but there was no choice but to take a good thing when I saw it or give up collecting altogether."

One suspects that her attitude to the men who were attracted to her was much the same.

Food is an easy metaphor: the symbol of a woman's care and nurturing of her family. Sooner or later, most diarists discuss food, including the women travelling to the American West. They often proudly describe the menu they manage to present and even the method they use to bake bread over a camp fire. Temporarily settled in Iowa, pioneer housewife Keturah Belknap describes the food she serves to twelve nice old ladies whom she invites to help her pick wool:

> June 20, 1842
>
> ... a fine chicken dinner, for cake I made a regular old fashioned pound cake like my mother used to make for weddings and now my name is out as a good cook so I am alright, for good cooking makes good friends.

Good cooking makes good friends. That's as memorable a

line as Frost's "Good fences make good neighbors," and just as fitting.

Nevada housewife Rachel Haskell wondered why she bothered to keep a diary, and in fact all that remains of it is about a month's worth of entries from 1867. She equates food directly with her family's well-being:

Sunday, 24th March
Didn't Mr. H excel himself in making a codfish balls [*sic*]—only he baked them in an entire cake in the oven. This with custard pie to top off with satisfied our inner man and we sat around the table till late in the evening all reading.... Their faces looked a pleasing sight as they ranged on opposite side of table from me, to a parent's eye....

A few days later, on the twenty-seventh, Haskell describes a visit from two gentlemen and a game of Authors with the whole family, followed by apples and gingerbread — a "spirited evening." Food and the table represent to Haskell the comfort and well-being of her family.

The lack of food also becomes an item to report and a symbol of deprivation for those diarists living through an ordeal, whether on a harsh trail or in prison or during wartime. Marie "Missie" Vassiltchikov (1917-1978), who survived in Berlin during World War Two, evokes an image of champagne, a sparkling metaphor for her own spirit. An aristocratic Russian emigrée with a Lithuanian passport, Vassiltchikov was trapped in Berlin at the outbreak of the war and kept a diary of events, not feelings. Yet her feelings emerge as her health and nerves are worn down. She admits to apprehension during the Berlin Blitz and later to a fear of being buried alive with no one knowing where she is.

On October 13, 1943, she and a friend throw a cocktail party with two bottles of wine and half a bottle of vermouth, hoping that their guests will contribute something: "[P]eople brought ice and champagne and we poured everything together, a weird mixture; but it was consumed without complaints."

On her twenty-seventh birthday in 1944, Vassiltchikov describes her morning in the underground of the Friedrichstrasse station during an air raid. In the evening she goes to Potsdam to visit friends, who surprise her with a birthday dinner: "much champagne, and a real cake with candles."

Escaping from her office work in Berlin, she manages to find a job in a hospital in Vienna just in time to experience the vicious air raids there. Hungry most of the time, nevertheless she celebrates her twenty-eighth birthday with a friend who arrives with — what else? — a bottle of champagne.

On the edge of starvation, she makes her way back to Germany, arriving in Munich on August 31, 1945: "Six years ago the war started," she writes on September 1. "It seems a lifetime."

Vassiltchikov escapes to the countryside with a woman friend; after they have suffered scarlet fever together, they arrive at another aristocratic friend's ruined castle. There she lives for a time in one of the gatehouses, attended by the family's retainers, eating fruit and vegetables from the farm — but no meat — and drinking vintage wine from the estate's cellars!

An earlier comment, on May 29, 1944, expresses her attitude: "[A]fter the frequent horrors of our daily life, every brief moment of relaxation and gaiety is a gift of the gods, which one tries to enjoy to the utmost."

Marie Vassiltchikov's moving account of her survival is as incongruous as champagne and as indomitable as the human spirit.

Less common metaphors can express the spirit of a woman and perhaps indicate that the diarist knows exactly what she is doing in a book of her own. Canadian artist Emily Carr (1871-1945), for example, uses a metaphor to spell out what her jotting means to her:

> Why call this manuscript *Hundred and Thousands*?
> Because it is made up of scraps of nothing, which,
> put together, made the trimming and furnished the
> sweetness for what might otherwise have been a
> drab life sucked away without crunch.... It was these
> tiny things that, collectively, taught me how to live.

That's what metaphors do: teach one how to live.

Sometimes human beings serve as the metaphor in a diarist's life. Henry Sidney Newcomer was his mother's metaphor for creation. Rebecca Kosier Newcomer (1863-1913) kept a journal of her first child's development from birth to age twenty-one. Her very last entry reveals her pride of creation:

May 3, 1908
Yesterday Harry was elected to Phi Beta Kappa
and telegraphed the good news to us last night.
Am I proud and delighted? Yes, why indeed, but
not surprised.

The puppy that self-explorer Alice Koller took with her to Nantucket when she retreated to find herself became her metaphor. She called it, not surprisingly, Logos. Koller had to train the pup, house-break him, take him for walks, help him with his teething, keep him healthy, and she finally perceived that she was using him. She writes, "Why did I think he'd be exempt from the stupid way I foul up relationships with people?" A metaphor can often be the source of unwelcome illumination.

Contemporary American doctor Michelle Harrison explains her use of a tape recorder: "In recent years, instead of writing in small thick journals, I switched to a tape recorder, both to save time and to use more creatively the time I spend driving to and from work." What it really provided her with was a buffer zone, a time of re-entry, both coming and going, from her difficult personal life as a single mother with not enough money and her disillusioning professional life as a woman doctor in a field dominated by men. Considering all the time she has spent with her tape recorder she realizes it has become "at times an almost human companion, to whom I unburdened myself at the end of the day." When Harrison decides to take a leave of absence, never to return, she confides to her electronic companion in the car seat: "As I drive to the hospital for these final twenty-four hours, I keep looking for a different ending."

New England spinster Alice James (1848-1892) knew all along that her diary was her metaphor: her diary was her self. She had early developed a detached view of herself as third person, possibly because she was truly a writer by nature, certainly because as an invalid she was a bystander and perpetual observer. Her diary was her only work and she took care to foster the persona she created for it. The real clue to what Alice's diary meant to her lies in her last act concerning it.

On March 6, 1892, Alice lay dying. Too weak to write for some time, she had been dictating. She asked her companion Katharine Loring to read back her last entry — and *corrected it*. Alice James's diary was going to stand for Alice James, so it had to be right.

"Metaphor," writes American English professor James Olney, "is essentially a way of knowing." When a diarist cannot seize a situation, she simplifies it by making something else stand for it, something she can know, comprehend, get a handle on. Thus, the diary itself is a metaphor. But what is the diary a metaphor of?

Metaphor, n. "A name or descriptive term is transferred to some object to which it is not properly applicable" (*The Oxford English Dictionary*).

Poets use metaphor as a method to describe by transference something that is, possibly, indescribable. Thus, "the moon is a lantern." The moon is not really a lantern, nor is it *like* a lantern — that would be a simile. The moon provides soft illumination at night and serves as a guide for our stumbling feet; therefore, because of these qualities it has in common with a lantern, the poet calls it a lantern.

Like the poet who cannot touch the moon or describe it, the diarist cannot touch her life or describe her self, yet she can see and resee, that is, reread her diary, and she can touch it, pick it up, write in it, weep in it, shut it, and put it away, all the while going about her inexorably daily life. She cannot know herself, not fully, but she can begin to see a pattern in her life, a path of her soul, and maybe even a dim outline of her self in her diary.

A woman's diary becomes, as it did for Alice James, a metaphor for the person. It becomes the projection of the diarist's psyche, one we may dare to examine. The diarist reflects inward from the diary-mirror to shine light on her work; gathering what she needs, she spins her thread of life from the diary-spindle; using the thread, she weaves her design on the diary-loom to create her individual web-story.

CHAPTER SIX

Spinning the Thread

WHEN A WOMAN SERIOUSLY ASKS HER-SELF WHAT IT MEANS TO BE A WOMAN SHE IS PULLING AT A THREAD THAT CAN UNRAVEL AN ENTIRE CULTURE.

Kim Chernin

Apart from the spinners and weavers of actual thread and cloth, who reported on their tasks completed, a number of diarists over the years have thought of themselves as spinning and compared themselves to a spider. Confederate Mary Chesnut, sitting helpless in the middle of that hateful war, wrote:

> March 11, 1861
> I think this journal will be disadvantageous for me,
> for I spend my time now like a spider spinning my
> own entrails instead of reading as my habit was at
> all spare moments.

Louisa May Alcott also compares herself to a spider, though not always gratefully: "November 29, 1856 ... rather tired of living like a spider, — spinning my brains out for money," but later she admits her need to be alone, to spin/create:

"October, 1872 I can't work at home and need to be alone to spin, like a spider."

In this century Etty Hillesum realizes how important it is to spin that thread:

> March, 1942
> [H]ere on these pages I am spinning my thread. And a thread does run through my life, through my reality, like a continuous line.... It's not so much the imperfect words on these faint blue lines, as the feeling, time and again, of returning to a place from which one can continue to spin one and the same thread, where one can gradually create a continuum, a continuum which is really one's life.

As feminist theologian Mary Daly says in her book *Gyn/Ecology*, "Spinsters spin and weave, mending and creating unity of consciousness."

We are all spinners. Diarists spin out their lives. The spider-spinner sits in the centre spinning out the words: diary as web. Sometimes the entire process requires a miracle, for the words to whirl, the world to turn, for diary truly to become more than thread, to become a lifeline in both senses — a line *from* life and a line *to* life.

All their lives women's eyes have been on men. They see themselves in men's eyes. They pattern their behaviour and gauge their moods and adapt their work and deal with their mothers and rear their children and communicate with others, always with at least one eye on what their men are doing, thinking, feeling — especially *feeling* because men seldom know themselves and women have to interpret for them.

This is what life means to a woman, no matter in which century. Even in this one, "free" as women are, inequities abound, slow to be balanced, and chains still rattle, slow to be unshackled. Women are still too dependent on men for favours and freedom, definition and acceptance, still too much in the keeping of men — not only in the keeping but in thrall, unable to see or hear themselves think. So far we haven't made enough noise to be heard — let alone listened to.

First, literacy was a tool women had to hone before they could write down what they were thinking. Then they had to see what they thought, hear themselves before they could find anything like a voice — albeit a private, paper one, more like a whisper. When diaries began to be public, they still weren't very. They might be circulated among the family, as Alice James requested hers be, or there might be a small print run produced by a vanity publishing house, or maybe someone in the business thought it would be interesting to publish Aunt Fanny's papers. In most cases, the audience was limited and erasure was swift and inexorable. Even today most women's diaries that are published quickly end up stacked on remainder tables or listed in out-of-print catalogues. Inflammatory pages don't raise heat when they're not opened to the air. Writing can be a subversive act but it doesn't subvert much if its light is hidden under a bushel. What if the bushel is a haystack and the diary is the thread on the invisible needle? Maybe.

In other centuries, women's diaries were never intended for publication; that's why they were allowed. Those
funny little early diaries were never intended to topple
governments. The diarists themselves hardly knew what
they were doing: just trying to put a handle on their lives,
recognize their labours, identify their pain, name their sorrows — joy, too. Dismissed as banal and unimportant, their
diaries were never torched, simply left untouched and
unread, undiscovered and undeciphered.

Women had no manuals to guide them from generation
to generation because their records were all but obliterated. Each generation had to re-invent the wheel — that is,
write new lines, draw a new map. Canadian feminist academic Helen Buss uses the map image in her book, *Mapping
Our Selves*, to chart Canadian women's autobiographical
writing. She thinks that map making offers "a dynamic
metaphor far superior to any offered by passive mirror gazing." The self and the world it exists in must both be
"mapped." The exploration turns inward; Ariadne's thread
leads in, through the maze, and out again. We are a-mazed
and need a map to find our way out!

A simpler metaphor: women's journals have been compared to crazy quilts, full of bits and pieces, created by hap-
penstance and using whatever was in the rag box. Today
quilts hang in art galleries and even seemingly haphazard
patterns are seen to have some design. So diaries are
acknowledged as part of the art form of lifewriting. Diary
as quilt.

The diary is actually more like a loom. Each spinner/weaver picks up her own threads and follows them. There are many threads to pick up, and they often end with a question.

American Evelyn Scott (a pseudonym for novelist Elsie Dunn, 1893-1963), ill after childbirth, hears another woman screaming in labour and asks a question that can rock a woman's world: "I wonder if this agony of birth is really all there is — if it is life — the basic thing — and if everything else is irrelevant." For Scott, perhaps it was. Scott's novel *Escapade* is based on the diary she kept when she eloped to Mexico with a married man. She was more famous in her day than William Faulkner and was asked to give him an affidavit; her books, however, fell out of print and only recently have been reprinted for a new generation of women readers.

Hungarian Hannah Senesh (1921-1944), claimed as a martyr to the cause of Jewish freedom, kept a questioning, introspective diary from her thirteenth year in Hungary, where she was born, to Palestine, where she moved and totally involved herself in Zionism. She asks herself too many questions she can't answer:

May 18, 1940
There are so many things I don't understand, least of all myself. I would like to know who and what I really am but I can only ask the questions, not answer them. Either I have changed a lot, or the world around me has changed. Or have the eyes with which I see myself changed?

Senesh volunteered for a dangerous mission to try to get some people out of Nazi-occupied Hungary, from which she never returned. In one of the last entries in her diary, while in training, her eyes open wider:

> September 19, 1943
> In my life's chain of events nothing was accidental. Everything happened according to an inner need.

When a woman starts asking the questions, as feminist writer Kim Chernin warns in her book, *Reinventing Eve*, the thread may start to unravel the entire culture. Katherine Mansfield started pulling at the thread in April 1920:

> [T]here are signs that we are intent as never before on trying to puzzle out, to live by, our own particular self. *Der Mensch muss frei sein* — free, disentangled, single. Is it not possible that the rage for confession, autobiography, especially for memories of earliest childhood, is explained by our persistent yet mysterious belief in a self which is continuous and permanent; which, untouched by all we acquire and all we shed, pushes a green spear through the dead leaves and through the mould, thrusts a scaled bud through years of darkness until, one day, the light discovers it and shakes the flower free and — we are alive — we are flowering for our moment upon the earth? This is the moment which, after all, we live for — the moment of direct feeling when we are most ourselves and least personal.

She was dying by that time; maybe she was able to see more clearly. Doomed and sick, Mansfield, who died in 1923 at the age of thirty-five, started pulling at her mask in Switzerland where she went to try to find a new, effective treatment for her tuberculosis.

Some time between November 1921–
January 1922:
So do we all begin by acting and the nearer we are to what we would be the more perfect our *disguise*. Finally there comes the moment when *we are no longer acting*; it may even catch us by surprise. We may look in amazement at our no longer borrowed plumage. The two have merged; that which we put on has joined that which was; acting has become action. The soul has accepted this livery for its own after a time of trying on and approving.

These are the kinds of lines women write in their diaries, asking questions, following threads as they weave in and out of their inner/outer lives. They record their tasks and their tales, their personal stories and their search. Each one's through-line is different, yet a thread of continuity guides them outward and forward to the point where women are publicly spinning it and using it to weave their own web-stories.

Mary Daly recalls another activity of the spinster (married or not). Besides spinning thread, ditto, ditto, ditto, she can spin a yarn. Women are spinning in their diaries, spinning yarn, spinning a yarn, weaving cloth, weaving a story, weaving a network of communication, weaving a web, enough to catch a life, hold a memory. If diary is truly a metaphor, assume a powerful one: a loom of one's own, on which the threads of the story are interwoven. The word *webster* originally meant a female weaver; *ster* was a female suffix, now most prominent in spinster. The diary/spinner/webster tells her stories in private to herself. She is the spider at the centre of her web, her own private domain. The silent secret place is always there, as close as a scrap of paper and a recalcitrant pen — private, trustworthy, invaluable.

Then, after the act of writing, after the recording, comes the rereading and the revision. Mary Jane Moffat and her co-editor, Charlotte Painter, rightly titled their book of diary excerpts *Revelations*. The revelations dazzle the diarists themselves, not only writers and artists but women from all walks of life. Some of them are highly articulate, others barely literate, yet they find expression in words on a page. The ink has thawed and it's no longer invisible.

American sociologist Elise Boulding speaks of the need of "storying," that is, of women telling one another their stories: mother to daughter, friend to friend, self to self. As women go about their daily business, they share tasks, endure hardships, pool resources, report news, exchange gossip. "There is a whole world of reverence and wonder in a dishpan," says Boulding. Even dishwater can be mystical and fabled. So can diaries.

The diary form itself is finally being taken seriously, as feminists have recognized one of the few means of expression available in other centuries to women of different backgrounds and education. No longer the sole domain of historians searching for mere details and the texture of everyday life, lifewriting, including epistolary scripts as well as journals, commands serious consideration by literary critics. They know that whether the words of a diary are sparse or abundant, the lines are there.

American novelist Joan Didion once commented on her writer's journal, comparing it to the bits and pieces that make up a ball of string. No piece of string was quite long enough to be useful yet it was too good to throw away. That's what the string, the thread, the lines in a diary are like. Length has almost nothing to do with their value. Short lines have their own truth to tell.

Accidents of life, tragic interruptions, disturbing distractions, unavoidable responsibilities have all stolen writing time from diarists and the time they needed to make their discoveries. Lack of opportunity, time, and privacy; modesty, reticence, and fear of discovery: all these factors have kept other diarists silent, or nearly so. Yet something comes through, the line from life, the lifeline.

Invalid writer Marie Lénéru, trapped in her own body, knew this better than most women. She recognized writing as her lifeline:

December, 1899
For me writing is a veritable reading of myself, in which I often meet with much more that is unexpected than in a book, even when it is original.... But what I read did not exist before. I put it there

when I discovered it....Thus one must write to
exist, to become one's self.

Is there a single key to the diary? Not the cheap brass one
that unlocks that tinny gilt catch. Women are tired of the
catch: the toe-stubbing, brain-numbing, heart-daunting
discrepancies between their words and men's interpreta-
tions of them. It remains to reread the writing of the past,
and to know it differently than before, not to pass on a tradition but to break its hold. If contemporary women have
reached the point where they can see what women are saying, seeing and being, then it is an amazing moment for the
writer as well as the reader.

Women have never paid much attention to themselves
because no one else does. This attitude is evident in
women's diaries because they have such difficulty disen-
tangling their perceptions from others' view of them, and
their voices from others' louder, authoritative ones, and
their words from others' language and interpretation. So
when a diarist has a crisis of identity or a moral struggle or
a sense of rage to deal with, she has to struggle to articulate her sense of self, having first to reject the litany and the
formulae that she has been handed and then to find her
own language and expression.

By reading through the censorship, interpreting the
litany, and going beyond the sometime passivity, tedium,
and banality of other diarists' lives and by reading instead
for the energy and devotion, the rage, passion, dedication,
the embracing of life, contemporary readers should be able

to discern the power and fascination of women's diaries and find the thread and the through-line. If they do, they're going to find out what it means to be a woman on this planet.

Bibliography

DIARIES

Alcott, Louisa May. *The Journals of Louisa May Alcott*. Joel Myerson and Daniel Shealy, eds. Boston: Little, Brown & Company, 1989.

Anonymous. *Go Ask Alice*. New York: Avon/Flare, 1982.

Bashkirtseff, Marie. *Marie Bashkirtseff: The Journal of a Young Artist*. Mary J. Serrano, trans. New York: E.P. Dutton & Co., 1923.

Bauman, Janina. *Winter in the Morning: A Young Girl's Life in the Warsaw Ghetto and Beyond, 1939-1945*. New York: The Free Press, 1986.

Berenson, Mary. *Mary Berenson: A Self-Portrait from Her Diaries and Letters*. Barbara Strachey and Jayne Samuels, eds. New York: W.W. Norton, 1983.

Bird, Isabella L. *A Lady's Life in the Rocky Mountains (1873)*. Norman: University of Oklahoma Press, 1988.

Brittain, Vera. *Wartime Chronicle: Vera Brittain's Diary, 1939-1945*. Alan Bishop and Y. Aleksandra Bennett, eds. London: Victor Gollancz Ltd., 1989.

Burney, Fanny. *Fanny Burney: Selected Letters and Journals*. Joyce Hemlow, ed. New York: Oxford University Press, 1987.

Carr, Emily. *Hundreds and Thousands*. Toronto: Clarke, Irwin, 1966.

Chesler, Phyllis. *With Child: A Diary of Motherhood*. New York: Thomas Y. Crowell, 1979.

Chesnut, Mary Boykin. *The Private Mary Chesnut: The Unpublished Civil War Diaries*. C. Vann Woodward and Elizabeth Muhlenfeld, eds. New York: Oxford University Press, 1984.

Chopin, Kate. *A Kate Chopin Miscellany*. Per Seyersted and Emily Toth, eds. Oslo: Universtetsforlaget; Natchitoches: Northwestern State University of Louisiana Press, 1979.

Culley, Margo. *A Day at a Time: The Diary Literature of American Women from 1764 to the Present*. New York: The Feminist Press, 1985.

Cullwick, Hannah. *The Diaries of Hannah Cullwick, Victorian Maidservant*. Liz Stanley, ed. New Brunswick, N.J.: Rutgers University Press, 1984.

Daibu, Lady. *The Poetic Memoirs of Lady Daibu*. Philip Tudor Harris, trans. Stanford, Calif.: Stanford University Press, 1980.

Danica, Elly. *Don't: A Woman's Word*. Charlottetown: Gynergy Books, 1988.

Dessaulles, Henriette. *Hopes and Dreams: The Diary of Henriette Dessaulles, 1874-1881*. Liedewy Hawke, trans. Willowdale, Ont.: Hounslow Press, 1971.

Dohaney, M.T. *When Things Get Back to Normal.* Porters Lake, N.S.: Pottersfield Press, 1989.

Dunbar-Nelson, Alice. *Give Us Each Day: The Diary of Alice Dunbar-Nelson.* Gloria T. Hull, ed. New York: W.W. Norton, 1984.

Field, Joanna (Marion Milner). *A Life of One's Own.* Los Angeles: J.P. Tarcher, Inc., 1981 (originally published 1936).

Filipovic, Zlata. *Zlata's Diary: A Child's Life in Sarajevo.* Christina Pribichevich-Zoric, trans. New York: Penguin Books, 1994.

Fountaine, Margaret. *Love Among the Butterflies: The Travels and Adventures of a Victorian Lady.* W.F. Cater, ed. London: Collins, 1980.

Frank, Anne. *Anne Frank: The Diary of a Young Girl.* New York: Pocket Books, Doubleday, 1968.

______. *The Diary of Anne Frank: The Critical Edition.* Prepared by The Netherlands State Institute for War Documentation. David Barnow and Gerrold Van der Stroom, eds. New York: Doubleday, 1989.

Franklin, Penelope. *Private Pages: Diaries of American Women, 1830s-1970s.* New York: Ballantine Books, 1986.

Graham, Elspeth, Hilary Hinds, Elaine Hobby, and Helen Wilcox. *Her Own Life: Autobiographical Writings by Seventeenth-Century Women.* London: Routledge, 1989.

Gregory, Lady Augusta. *Journals*. Daniel J. Murphy, ed. New York: Oxford University Press, 1978.

Halpern, Daniel, ed. *Our Private Lives: Journals, Notebooks, and Diaries*. New York: Vintage Books, Random House, 1990.

Hampsten, Elizabeth. *Read This Only to Yourself: The Private Writings of Midwestern Women, 1880-1910*. Bloomington: Indiana University Press, 1982.

Harrison, Michelle. *A Woman in Residence*. Toronto: Penguin Books, 1983.

Hillesum, Etty. *An Interrupted Life: The Diaries of Etty Hillesum, 1941-1943*. New York: Washington Square Press, 1985.

Horner, Joyce. *That Time of Year: A Chronicle of Life in a Nursing Home*. Amherst: The University of Massachusetts Press, 1982.

James, Alice. *The Diary of Alice James*. Leon Edel, ed. New York: Penguin Books, 1982.

Koller, Alice. *An Unknown Woman: A Journey to Self-Discovery*. Toronto: Bantam Books, 1988.

Kollwitz, Käthe. *The Diary and Letters of Käthe Kollwitz*, Hans Kollwitz, ed. Evanston, Ill.: Northwestern University Press, 1989.

Langton, Anne. *A Gentlewoman in Upper Canada: The Journals of Anne Langton*. H.H. Langton, ed. Toronto: Irwin Publishing, 1950.

Lau, Evelyn. *Runaway: Diary of a Street Kid*. Toronto: Harper Collins, 1989.

Lavell, Martha, The Diary of. The Sophia Smith Collection, Smith College, Northampton, Mass.

Le Guin, Magnolia Wynn. *A Home-Concealed Woman: The Diaries of Magnolia Wynn LeGuinn, 1901-1913*. Charles A. LeGuin, ed. Athens: University of Georgia Press, 1990.

Lénéru, Marie. *Journal of Marie Lénéru*. New York: The Macmillan Company, 1923.

Lensink, Judy Nolte, ed. *"A Secret to be Burried": The Diary and Life of Emily Hawley Gillespie, 1858-1888*. Iowa City: University of Iowa Press, 1989.

Lindbergh, Anne Morrow. *Bring Me a Unicorn: Diaries and Letters of Anne Morrow Lindbergh, 1922-1928*. New York: New American Library, 1973.

Logan, Deborah Norris, The Diary of. The Historical Society of Pennsylvania, Philadelphia, Penn.

Luchetti, Cathy, in collaboration with Carol Olwell. *Women of the West*. St. George, Utah: Antelope Island Press, 1982.

MacLane, Mary. *The Story of Mary MacLane, by Herself*. Chicago: Herbert S. Stone, 1902.

______. *I, Mary MacLane: A Diary of Human Days*. New York: Frederick A. Stokes Co., 1917.

Mansfield, Katherine. *The Letters and Journals of Katherine Mansfield*. Harmondsworth: Penguin Books, 1988.

Mead, Margaret. *An Anthropologist at Work: Writings of Ruth Benedict*. Boston: Houghton Mifflin, 1959.

Michitsuna, the mother of. *The Gossamer Years*. Edward Seidensticker, trans. Tokyo: Charles E. Tuttle, 1964.

Miller, Alice. Preface to *A Young Girl's Diary*. Daniel Gunn and Patrick Guyomard, eds. New York: Anchor Books, Doubleday, 1990.

Milner, Marion. *Eternity's Sunrise, A Way of Keeping a Diary*. London: Virago Press, 1989.

Modersohn–Becker, Paula. *Paula Modersohn-Becker: The Letters and Journals*. Arthur S. Wensinger and Carole Clew Hoey, trans. and eds. New York: Taplinger Publishing, 1983.

Moffat, Mary Jane, and Charlotte Painter, eds. *Revelations: Diaries of Women*. New York: Vintage Books, Random House, 1975.

Montgomery, Lucy Maud. *The Selected Journals of L.M. Montgomery, Vols. 1-3*. Mary Rubio and Elizabeth Waterston, eds. Toronto: Oxford University Press, 1985.

Morris, Mary. *Nothing to Declare: Memoirs of a Woman Traveling Alone*. New York: Penguin Books, 1988.

Murrell, Hilda. *Nature Diaries, 1961-1983*. Charles Sinker, ed. London: Collins, 1987.

Newcomer, Rebecca Kosier. *A Mother's Journal for Her Son, 1887-1908*. Marilyn Yalom, ed. Santa Barbara, Calif.: Capra Press, 1988.

Nijo, Lady. *The Confessions of Lady Nijo*. Karen Brazell, trans. Stanford, Calif.: Stanford University Press, 1973.

O'Bryon, Eleanor Dart. *Coming Home from Devil Mountain*. Tucson, Ariz.: Harbinger House, 1989.

Peet, Azalia Emma, The Diary of. The Sophia Smith Collection, Smith College, Northampton, Mass.

Plath, Sylvia. *The Journals of Sylvia Plath*. Ted Hughes and Frances McCullough, eds. New York: Ballantine Books, 1982.

Potter, Beatrix. *The Journal of Beatrix Potter, from 1881 to 1897*. Transcribed from her coded writings by Leslie Linder. London: Frederick Warne & Co., 1966.

Pym, Barbara. *A Very Private Eye: An Autobiography in Diaries and Letters*. Hazel Holt and Hilary Pym, eds. New York: E.P. Dutton, 1984.

Rinser, Luise. *Prison Journal*. Michael Hulse, trans. London: Macmillan, 1987.

Robinson, Jane. *Wayward Women: A Guide to Women Travellers*. New York: Oxford University Press, 1991.

Sand, George. *The Intimate Journal*. Marie Jenney Howe, trans. and ed. Chicago: Academy Chicago Publishers, 1984.

Sarton, May. *Journal of a Solitude: The Intimate Diary of a Year in the Life of a Creative Woman*. New York: W.W. Norton, 1977.

______. *The House by the Sea: A Journal*. New York: W.W. Norton, 1981.

______. *Recovering: A Journal*. New York: W.W. Norton, 1986.

______. *At Seventy: A Journal*. New York: W.W. Norton, 1987.

______. *After the Stroke: A Journal*. New York: W.W. Norton, 1990.

______. *Encore: A Journal of the Eightieth Year*. New York: W.W. Norton & Company, 1993.

Schäffer, Mary T.S. *Old Indian Trails of the Canadian Rockies*. New York: G.P. Putnam's Sons, 1911.

Schlissel, Lillian. *Women's Diaries of the Westward Journey*. New York: Schocken Books, 1982.

Schreiber, Le Anne. *Midstream: The Story of a Mother's Death and a Daughter's Renewal*. New York: Viking, 1990.

Scott, Evelyn. *Escapade: An Autobiography*. New York: Carroll & Graf Publishers, 1987.

Scott-Maxwell, Florida. *The Measure of My Days*. New York: Alfred A. Knopf, 1979.

Senesh, Hannah. *Hannah Senesh: Her Life and Diary*. New York: Schocken Books, 1973.

Shonagon, Sei. *The Pillow Book of Sei Shonagon*. Ivan Morris, ed. and trans. Harmondsworth: Penguin Books, 1967.

Smart, Elizabeth. *Necessary Secrets: The Journals of Elizabeth Smart*. Alice Van Wart, ed. Toronto: Deneau, 1986.

Smith, Elizabeth. *A Woman with a Purpose: The Diaries of Elizabeth Smith, 1872-1884*. Veronica Strong-Boag, ed. Toronto: University of Toronto Press, 1980.

"Taylor, Marion," The Diary. of The Schlesinger Library, Radcliffe College, Cambridge, Massachusetts.

Thaxter, Celia. *An Island Garden*. Boston: Houghton Mifflin Company, 1894.

Thompson, Tierl, ed. *Dear Girl: The Diaries and Letters of Two Working Women, 1897-1917*. London: The Women's Press, 1987.

Tolstoy, Sophia. *The Diaries of Sophia Tolstoy*. Cathy Porter, trans. New York: Random House, 1985.

Truitt, Anne. *Daybook: The Journal of an Artist*. New York: Penguin Books, 1988.

______. *Turn: The Journal of an Artist*. New York: Penguin Books, 1986.

Ulrich, Laurel Thatcher. *A Midwife's Tale: The Life of Martha Ballard, Based on Her Diary*. New York: Alfred A. Knopf, 1990.

Vassiltchikov, Marie "Missie." *The Berlin Diaries, 1940-1945.* London: The Folio Society, 1991.

Wainwright, Sonny. *Stage V: A Journal Through Illness.* Berkeley, Calif.: Acacia Books, 1984.

Warren, Mary, and T.S. Schaeffer. *A Hunter of Peace: Old Indian Trails of the Canadian Rockies.* E.J. Hart, ed. Banff, Alta.: The Whyte Foundation, 1980.

Webb, Beatrice. *Glitter Around and Darkness Within.* Vol. One: 1873-1892. Norman and Jeanne MacKenzie, eds. Cambridge, Mass.: The Belknap Press of Harvard University Press, 1982.

______. *All the Good Things of Life.* Vol. Two: 1892-1905. Norman and Jeanne MacKenzie, eds. Cambridge, Mass.: The Belknap Press of Harvard University Press, 1983.

Whiting, Ethel Robertson, The Diary of. Private collection. Microfil copy in the Bancroft Library.

Woolf, Virginia. *The Diary of Virginia Woolf,* Vols. 1-5. Anne Olivier Bell, ed., assisted by Andrew McNeillie. New York: Harcourt Brace Jovanovich, 1977-1984.

______. *A Passionate Apprentice; The Early Journals, 1897-1909.* Mitchell A. Leaska, ed. Toronto: Lester & Orpen Dennys/New York: Harcourt Brace Jovanovich, 1990.

______. *A Room of One's Own.* New York: A Harvest/HBJ Book, Harcourt Brace Jovanovich, London, 1929.

_____. *A Writer's Diary*. Harper/Collins: Triad Grafton Books, 1953.

Wordsworth, Dorothy. *The Grasmere Journal*. New York: Henry Holt & Company, 1987.

DIARY EXCERPTS

Alexander, Jo, et al., eds. *Women and Aging: An Anthology by Women*. Corvallis, Ore.: Calyx Books, 1986.

Bank, Mirra. *Anonymous Was a Woman*. New York: St. Martin's Press, 1979.

Blodgett, Harriet. *Centuries of Female Days: Englishwomen's Private Diaries*. New Brunswick, N.J.: Rutgers University Press, 1988.

Blodgett, Harriet, ed. *The Englishwoman's Diary: An Anthology*. London: Fourth Estate, Cambridge University Press, 1992.

Blythe, Ronald, ed. *The Pleasures of Diaries*. New York: Pantheon Books, 1989.

Fischer, Christine, ed. *Women in the American West, 1849-1900: Let Them Speak for Themselves*. New York: E.P. Dutton, 1978.

Hampsten, Elizabeth. *Read This Only to Yourself: The Private Writings of Midwestern Women, 1880-1910*. Bloomington: Indiana University Press, 1982.

Holliday, Laurel, ed. *Heart Songs: The Intimate Diaries of Young Girls*. Guerneville, Calif.: Bluestocking Books, 1978.

Lifshin, Lyn, ed. *Ariadne's Thread: A Collection of Contemporary Women's Journals*. New York: Harper & Row, 1982.

Mallon, Thomas. *A Book of One's Own: People and Their Diaries*. New York: Penguin Books, 1987.

Niederman, Sharon, ed. *A Quilt of Words: Women's Diaries, Letters & Original Accounts of Life in the Southwest, 1860-1960*. Boulder, Colo.: Johnson Books, 1990.

Rogers, Katharine M., and William McCarthy. *The Meridian Anthology of Early Women Writers: British Literary Women from Aphra Behn to Maria Edgeworth, 1660-1800*. New York: New American Library, 1987.

Rosenblatt, Paul C. *Bitter, Bitter Tears: Nineteenth-Century Diaries and Twentieth-Century Grief Theories*. Minneapolis: University of Minnesota Press, 1983.

HISTORY

Anderson, Bonnie S., and Judith P. Zinsser. *A History of Her Own: Women in Europe from Pre-History to the Present*, Vols I & II. New York: Harper & Row, 1988.

Ariès, Philippe, André Bejin, and Georges Duby, eds. *A History of Private Life: Revelations of the Medieval World*. Cambridge, Mass.: The Belknap Press of Harvard University Press, 1988.

______. *A History of Private Life: Passions of the Renaissance.* Cambridge, Mass.: The Belknap Press of Harvard University Press, 1989.

D'Emilio, John, and Estelle B. Freedman. *Intimate Matters: A History of Sexuality in America.* New York: Harper & Row, 1988.

Dinnerstein, Dorothy. *The Mermaid and the Minotaur: Sexual Arrangements and Human Malaise.* New York: Harper Colophon Books, 1977.

Douglas, Ann. *The Feminization of American Culture.* New York: Alfred A. Knopf, 1977.

Frankl, Victor E. *Man's Search for Meaning.* New York: Simon & Schuster, 1962.

Helsinger, Elizabeth K., Robin Lauterbach Sheets, and William Veeder. *The Woman Question, Volume I: Defining Voices.* Chicago: The University of Chicago Press, 1989.

______. *The Woman Question, Volume II: Literary Issues.* Chicago: University of Chicago Press, 1989.

Spender, Dale. *Man Made Language.* London: Pandora, 1980.

______. *Women of Ideas, and what men have done to them.* London: Pandora Press, Unwin Hyman, 1982.

Stanton, Domna C., ed. *The Female Autograph: Theory and Practice of Autobiography from the Tenth to the Twentieth Century.* Chicago: The University of Chicago Press, 1987.

THEORY

Belenky, Mary Field, Blythe McVicker Clinchy, Nancy Rule Goldberger, and Jill Mattuck Tarule. *Women's Ways of Knowing: The Development of Self, Voice, and Mind*. New York: Basic Books, 1986.

Benstock, Shari, ed. *The Private Self: Theory and Practice of Women's Autobiographical Writings*. Chapel Hill: University of North Carolina Press, 1988.

Berger, John. *Ways of Seeing*. London: BBC and Penguin Books, 1985.

Bernard, Jessie. *The Future of the Marriage*. New York: World Publishing, 1972.

Bernikow, Louise. *Among Women*. New York: Harper Colophon, 1981.

Boulding, Dr. Elise. *Learning and the Familial Society: The Place of Family in Times of Transition*. Public Lecture and Seminar, University of British Columbia, March 19, 1981; The Vanier Institute of the Family, Ottawa, 1981.

Brodzki, Bella, and Celeste Schenck. *Life/Lines: Theorizing Women's Autobiography*. Ithaca, N.Y.: Cornell University Press, 1988.

Brownmiller, Susan. *Femininity*. New York: Simon & Schuster, 1984.

Brownstein, Rachel M. *Becoming a Heroine: Reading About Women in Novels*. New York: Penguin Books, Viking Press, 1984.

Buss, Helen M. *Mapping Our Selves*. Montreal & Kingston: McGill-Queen's University Press, 1993.

Chernin, Kim. *Reinventing Eve: Modern Women in Search of Herself*. New York: Perennial Library, Harper & Row, 1988.

Chesler, Phyllis. *Women and Madness*. New York: Avon, 1973.

Daly, Mary. *Gyn/Ecology: The Metaethics of Radical Feminism*. Boston: Beacon Press, 1978.

______. *Websters' First New Intergalactic Wickedary of the English Language*. Boston: Beacon Press, 1987.

Gilligan, Carol. *In a Different Voice: Psychological Theory and Women's Development*. Cambridge, Mass.: Harvard University Press, 1983.

Griffin, Susan. *Woman and Nature: The Roaring Inside Her*. New York: Harper Colophon, 1978.

Heilbrun, Carolyn G. *Reinventing Womanhood*. New York: W.W. Norton, 1979.

______. *Writing a Woman's Life*. New York: W.W. Norton, 1988.

Irigaray, Luce. *Speculum of the Other Woman*. Gillian C. Gill, trans. Ithaca, N.Y.: Cornell University Press, 1985.

Josselson, Ruthellen. *Finding herself: Pathways to Identity Development in Women*. San Francisco: Josey-Bass Publishers, 1990.

Kome, Penney. *Somebody Has to Do It: Whose Work Is Housework?* Toronto: McClelland & Stewart, 1982.

Lerner, Harriet Goldhor. *The Dance of Anger*. New York: Perennial, Harper & Row, 1986.

Miller, Jean Baker. *Toward a New Psychology of Women*. Boston: Beacon Press, 1986.

Olney, James. *Metaphors of Self: The Meaning of Autobiography*. Princeton, N.J.: Princeton University Press, 1981.

Olsen, Tillie. *Silences*. New York: Delta/Seymour Lawrence, 1979.

The Personal Narratives Group, eds. *Interpreting Women's Lives: Feminist Theory and Personal Narratives*. Bloomington: Indiana University Press, 1989.

Spacks, Patricia Meyer. *Gossip*. Chicago: The University of Chicago Press, 1986.

Stanton, Domna C. ed. *The Female Autograph: Theory and Practice of Autobiography from the Tenth to the Twentieth Century*. Chicago: The University of Chicago Press, 1987.

Walker, Barbara G. *The Crone*. New York: Perennial Library, Harper & Row, 1988.

Weldon, Fay. *Letters to Alice: On First Reading Jane Austen*. London: Coronet Books, Hodder & Stoughton, 1984.

Index